T0077939

OVERCOMING THE STORMS

PAUL PHILLIPS

authorHOUSE®

AuthorHouse™
1663 Liberty Drive
Bloomington, IN 47403
www.authorhouse.com
Phone: 833-262-8899

Published by AuthorHouse 10/06/2020

ISBN: 978-1-7283-6998-3 (sc)
ISBN: 978-1-7283-7017-0 (e)

Print information available on the last page.

Any people depicted in stock imagery provided by Getty Images are models, and such images are being used for illustrative purposes only. Certain stock imagery © Getty Images.

This book is printed on acid-free paper.

Scripture quotations marked KJV are from the Holy Bible, King James Version (Authorized Version). First published in 1611. Quoted from the KJV Classic Reference Bible, Copyright © 1983 by The Zondervan Corporation.

Scripture quotations marked NKJV are taken from the New King James Version. Copyright © 1982 by Thomas Nelson, Inc. Used by permission. All rights reserved.

Scripture quotations marked AMP are from The Amplified Bible, Old Testament copyright © 1965, 1987 by the Zondervan Corporation. The Amplified Bible, New Testament copyright © 1954, 1958, 1987 by The Lockman Foundation. Used by permission. All rights reserved.

Unless otherwise indicated, all scripture quotations are from The Holy Bible, English Standard Version® (ESV®). Copyright ©2001 by Crossway Bibles, a division of Good News Publishers. Used by permission. All rights reserved.

Scripture quotations marked NIV are taken from the Holy Bible, New International Version®. NIV®. Copyright © 1973, 1978, 1984 by International Bible Society. Used by permission of Zondervan. All rights reserved. [Biblica]

To:

_____

From:

_____

Date:

_____

Ye are of God, little children, and have overcome
them: because greater is he that is in you, than
he that is in the world (1 John 4:4kjv).

CONTENTS

A FEW OF MY PERSONAL
MIRACLE'S AND STORMS

Miracles:

*In the year of 2004, I suffered a Massive <u>Seizure which left me in a coma for over seven days</u> which almost took my life. Doctors had given up on me ever recovering and advised my wife that I was brain dead and if I did come out of the coma that I would live a life like a vegetable. But God, stepped in and woke me up from the coma and restored my life back to me leaving doctors confused.

*In the year of 2008, my daughter and I were involved in a Head on <u>Collision with another vehicle. We were driving from my daughters nursing class going straight on the highway. This lady had to cross over our lane in order for her to get to the highway. I guess she did not see us </u>coming but when she turned and crossed over our lane to get to the highway, she slammed directly head on into us. My head was smashed into the windshield and my daughter was knocked unconscious. From the look of our vehicles, you would have thought that no one could have possibly survived from it. Doctors pulled glass particles out of my forehead. My daughter suffered injuries as well. But, by God's grace what could have been fatal we both survived.

Storms:

*2014 was probably one of the hardest years I have ever had to experience or endure in my life. That particular year I lost my Father. He had been sick for some time, but the family had found ways of dealing with the various stages of Parkinson's disease and his gradual downward spiral in his health. Actually, I felt that as his life was coming to an end that I would be the strong one in the family and that I would be prepared for that day when it finally came. When I did get the call that my father has passed it seemed like it was a first time ever hearing of his illness not to mention a shock of him dying. My mind as well as my body froze like never before. I could not breath, talk or even think. At that very moment I began thinking about our life together and what it was going to be like without my father around. Depression, loneliness, and all kind of dreadful thoughts took over me. Without the help of God and the support of my family in no way could I have made it through that period of time.

*1995, was the year that my wife and I after two years of struggling and trying to get a Home Loan we finally got approved! We knew how much money we had to work with, we knew what type of home we were going to have built. We even knew the very spot where the home was going to be built. Because we had so much time to prepare, by the time the house was going to be built we had brought and paid for everything needed to fill the entire house completely! In order for us to get the extremely low interest rate, the bank had given us a time frame as to when the house was to start and the date when it was expected to be completed As the time frame was coming to an end, the house was only a third completed. My wife and I was devastated at the thought of losing the loan and living back in the apartment the very one we so longed to leave. Through a lot of prayers and God stepping in, on the very last day of the loan agreement the builder and the loan officer worked it out and the loan time frame got extended. God knows our needs and our heart and will step-in right-on time, every time!

To God, You are the head of my life. Without You none of my existence would even be possible. Lord, You have brought me through so many trials and many even the doctors still do not understand my healings. I thank you Lord for giving me life, wisdom, peace and joy in writing the goodness of who You are! You are my all and all and my everything!

To my beautiful and lovely Wife of more than thirty-four glorious years. Elaina, you are indeed a true Proverbs 31 Woman of God! You are my rock, and my constant encourager! You have stood by my side through the good times and the not so good times and everything that I have ever endured or tried to achieve! I thank you for constantly pushing me to strive for more and never allowing me to sit still! Thank you for being my biggest supporter and most of all, I thank you for always loving me!

To my three gorgeous Daughter's Tanisha, Jocelyn and Amber. I Thank you, three women of God, for being patient with Dad and answering all my crazy questions and singing to me a comfortable song to relax me. I am so proud of the beautiful women you three have become. Stay strong in the Lord and He will continue to guild you!

To my seven Grand Children:

Julius Morris Jr., Johnathan Morris, Jeremiah Morris, Joshua Bunting, Joseph Bunting, Amina Okoth and Nia Okoth. The number 7 is perfection! I am excited to see what the Good Lord has in store for each of you. Never give up on your dreams and goals in life, believe me, they can be achieved! Nothing is too hard for GOD! Keep on making PaPa smile.

MANY ARE THE AFFLICTIONS
OF THE RIGHTEOUS,
BUT THE LORD DELIVERED
THEM OUT OF THEM ALL

(Psalms 34:17kjv).

INTRODUCTION

Every one of us at one time or another have experienced some type of Storm or Affliction in our lifetime that has made such an impact on us that has either affected or altered our future plans or current situation. As long as you are breathing, you are either coming out of a struggle or getting ready to go into one. To overcome a particular life storm or struggle, there has to be one to overcome. Storms can come in the form of feelings of depression, loneliness, a sudden illness, a bad breakup or even the loss of a loved one. Of course, we will face challenges and heartaches while going through life but, the question is how will you respond when it happens to you? I know it is hard for someone to completely understand your situation especially if they have not experienced it and have gone through it before themselves.

If someone is trying hard to console you after you have just lost a loved one, how can they say that they understand your situation if they have never lost a loved one before? Say you are experiencing heartache from a recent nasty divorce; can you truly be consoled from one who has never been divorced? Well, I am here to tell you that after all the pain, after all the disappointments and heartaches, you do have reassurance that you will come out on top and just fine because it tells us so right there in the Bible.

Apostle Paul states in (2Tim 3:10-12kjv):

"But thou hast fully known my doctrine, manner of life, purpose, faith, longsuffering, charity, patience, persecutions, afflictions, which came unto me at Antioch, at Iconium, at Lystra; what persecutions I endured: but out of them all the Lord delivered me."

Just look around and think about all the negativity, the pain, and the heartaches that you have had to experience just within the past year itself. You can honestly raise your hands and look the enemy straight in the face and say, "You tried to defeat me, you tried to take me down and out, but look at me, I'm still standing! I am still here! You did not win! satin, you did not win!!"

Many have endured and experienced the very same storms and battles that we are experiencing even today but the Lord delivered them, and the same Lord will protect you and will deliver and keep you as well. My dear reader, storms of life will come but with the Lord on our side, you can make it! You are an overcomer and you will come out as pure gold.

CHAPTER 1

WHO AM I?

"Therefore, if any man be in Christ, he is a new
creature: old things are passed away; behold all things
are become new (2 Corinthians 5:17kjv).

If you ask the average person, the question "Tell me about yourself."
They will probably tell you something like, "Well, I work at the local
plant, I am married, and I have four children." But when you really
want to know who a person is, I guess you will ask a more personal
question like "Who are you?" Then they will probably give you a
more personal answer like giving you their name, where they live
and so on.

We find in the eighth chapter of the book of Mark where Jesus
asked his disciples, "Whom do men say that I am?" And they
answered, John the Baptist: but some say, Elias; and others, One of
the prophets (Mark 8:27-28kjv). Then Jesus asked the disciples, "But
whom say ye that I am?" And Peter answered and saith unto him,
"Thou art the Christ" (Mark 8:29kjv). Peter indeed did say the right
answer, "The anointed One, The Messiah."

I ask you my dear reader, "Who do people say you are?" Main
question is what do you say about yourself? Do you even know who
you are? If the question was asked to you "Who are you" and your

first response was your name, address, occupation, kids and so on, you have missed the point. Fact of the matter is that so many of us have simply forgotten who we are! We have lowered our standards towards life. There used to be a time in your life when going to church was not a debatable issue. There used to be a time in your life when the people you associated with were more like your standards and now you are trying to fit in with the in crowd. Whatever happen to your standards? Who are you? First and foremost, I know that I am a child of God and everything else falls after that, period.

We go through so many difficult struggles in life. We go through so many different times of hardships whether it be finances, family, spiritual, health that as time has gone by, we have lost that relationship we once had with Christ and has put other things ahead of Him. Every test that you may face, the Lord will provide a way out!

Have you forgotten who Jesus is? Maybe you have forgotten who he is, what he has done and what He stands for. Before you can do, say, ask of anything of the Lord, you must know who Christ is! Let me remind you that Jesus is perfect in all his ways. Jesus is the true and living God and our Savior. Christ has given you keys of authority, Christ has given you keys to make things happen and Christ the son of the living God has the keys to unlock heaven! You are a child of the King and you must understand:

> *Who you are- A born again Christian
> *Your Position-You have Authority
> *Your Relationship-You are a Child of the King!

You must remember that you have the DNA of the Father and that He loves you, He favors you and that you are under His covering. You are royalty and a Child of the King! You have the authority to tell the enemy to GO! No weapon formed against you will ever prosper. You can command unwanted spirits to take it's is hand off of your family, off of your finances, off of your life! Never forget who you are!

"...And have put on the new man, which is renewed in knowledge after the image of him that created him: Where there is neither Greek nor, circumcision nor uncircumcision, Barbarian, Scythian, bond nor free: but Christ is all, and all. Put on therefore, as the elect of God, holy and beloved, bowels of mercies, kindness, humbleness of mind, meekness, longsuffering"

(Colossians 3:10-12nkjv).

Many years ago, when my children were young, we homeschooled all three of them. My wife and I were very adamant about their education. We taught them and everything was spiritually based. Many people felt that we were depriving them from friends, parties, and mostly public-school activities. We began to allow them to attend a few public-school activities such as field trips, Black History contest and so on. Through time they gained friends. My youngest daughter who was around the age of five asked a question that threw my wife and I completely off balance and made us think. She said, "Mom and Dad, I don't understand something. You teach us to be kind to people, you teach us to be respectful especially to adults, you teach us to treat people the way we want to be treated but every so often you send us into the Lions den." My wife and I looked at each other with surprise wondering how these words could come from a five-year-old child.

My daughter then said that "When we go on field trips with the school and participate in their activities those kids are bad. They cuss, they fight each other and talk back to the teachers and I feel like I am in the Lion's den when I am around them. I get picked on when I don't act like them and I don't want to go back." I told Amber that

> But ye are a chosen generation, a royal priesthood, a holy nation, a peculiar people; that ye should shew forth the praises of him who hath called you out of darkness into his marvelous light (1 Peter 2:9kjv).

3

"you don't have to change for anyone. You stay exactly who you are. You are a good girl and a good person, and it is ok that other children don't like you for who you are."

I have heard my same daughter saying those exact same words to her daughters. If you find yourself being one way around certain people and you are being someone else when you are around others, you are not being fair and true to yourself. Why do you feel that you have to change for people? Have you ever asked yourself "Why am I acting like this" when you are in the presence of certain people? Do you feel that you are not good enough when around certain people? You have to pretend and speak a certain way in order to be accepted. Do you feel that you will not be liked if you just simply be yourself? Have you forgotten who you are? Have you lost your own personal identity? Tell me, who is that important that you have to be someone else to be around them? Maybe perhaps you are fellowshipping with the wrong crowd or people.

Why won't they accept you for who you are? What is going on with you? Are you not tired of trying to be someone who you are not to get something from someone who will probably never give you what you want! Sometimes we have to remind ourselves not so much as to who we are but whose we are!

> "But ye are a chosen generation, a royal priesthood, a holy nation, His own special people, that you may proclaim the praises of Him who called you out of darkness into His marvelous light" (1Peter 2:9kjv).

We are created and made in the image of God (Gen. 1:27kjv). My friend you are special in the sight of Christ. You were chosen by Him. Stay your mind on Christ, stay your focus on Him. Forget all the negativity of the world. Most of all find your peace in the Lord.

Prayer:

Dear Heavenly Father, I come to you asking for forgiveness. I have been through so much in life and I have suffered so much that I have not only lost sight of myself but I have lost sight of You Lord! I ask You to take away the burdens in my life and give me new hope and new visions and purpose in life. Today, I declare a breakthrough in my life! I declare, no more suffering with the spirit of doubt or confusion! No more allowing the enemy to step into my life! Never again will I allow myself to forget where I came from but more importantly, Father please never let me forget my first love which is You Lord! In Jesus name I pray, Amen.

Reflection and Chapter Questions

1. What is your response when someone ask you "Who are you?"
2. Do certain people affect your behavior?
3. In what ways have you found your true identity?
4. Why do you feel that Jesus asked his disciples, "But whom say ye that I am?"
5. Jesus is our creator, "In what ways can you relate to the mind of Christ to your own personality?

RSEARCH QUESTION:

When Jesus, said, "Get behind Me, Satin! For you are not mindful of the things of God, but the things of men." Who was Jesus referring to?

Note: You can find the answer at the end of the book

CHAPTER 2

WHOSE VOICE ARE YOU LISTENING TO?

"Call unto me and I will answer thee and shew thee
great and mighty things" (Jeremiah 33:3kjv).

W hen I was a child, my parents would often speak to me especially
my Dad who would on occasionally sit me down on the couch and
we would have these long talks about life which I despised! He would
say things like, "Junior one day you are going to become a man and
you are going to have to take on a lot of responsibilities" or "Junior,
one day your mom and dad are not going to be here to get you out
of situations and you will be held accountable for your thoughts,
words and actions."

Sometimes my Dad would talk to me for so long that I would
actually start crying for no reason at all. I remember thinking to
myself, Dad please just give me a spanking and take me out of my
misery but, he always stated that the talks were not a punishment
but were words of wisdom to live by. As I grew older and the talks
began to become far and in between, I could hear Dad's voice in
my head acting as advice especially when I went off to college and
I was all by myself. The voice of my Dad is still clear to me even as

a grown married man with three daughters, son in laws and seven grandchildren. The words that as a child I despised are actually words of wisdom that I have passed down to my daughters and they have passed down to their children.

Sometimes we hear voices coming in from all different sides and directions not knowing what to take in or believe. We get advice on how to eat, on how to treat people and even on how to raise our own children. Many times, it is very hard to believe or decipher what is best for the present situation. When our children were much younger, my wife and I decided to Homeschool our three daughters. Many people even close relatives would often tell us that we were depriving our children from parties, friends, and a social life. At that time, we had to go against the popular opinion of education. We truly had very little support homeschooling our children but we both had heard from the Lord that it was the best way to educate our children. We had a conformation one day when my youngest daughter came home from public school at the age of about five and said, "I am not going back, I'm sorry but yall have got to homeschool me" and the rest is history.

Why is it important that we hear voices? Actually, the only voice and the most important one is hearing the voice of the Lord. Before making any big or important decisions, we always try to pray on it in agreement with each other and most importantly hearing a word from the Lord. Sometimes after praying the Lord will speak to us and have us to look at situations from a totally different aspect from where we were approaching it from. How do you know that you are actually hearing the voice of the Lord and not from your own conscious? Jesus says that:

"My sheep hear my voice and I know them, and they follow me" (John 10:27kjv).

The Bible also says that:

"The Lord is my shepherd; I shall not want" (Psalms 23:1 kjv). Meaning that when the Lord is your Shepherd, you will want for nothing.

Now, when you think of a sheep, how would you describe it? Well, a sheep is helpless, defenseless, and totally dependent upon the shepherd for protection and everything else. Truthfully, in this world we live in today with so much violence and unpredictable people I can relate to the sheep. At many times I feel defenseless

> Call unto me and I will answer thee and shew thee great and mighty things (Jeremiah 33:3kjv).

and I must depend on the Lord for my protection. I know His voice and I can distinguish it from everything else. His voice is clear, sometimes loud, and is always directly to the point. There is no wavering, not doubting or debating between voices.

In that same verse it says:

"Thou preparest a table before me in the presence of mine enemies" (Psalms 23:5kjv).

Even while being in the midst of wolves who are desperately wanting to devour and eat them up, the sheep can eat in peace, the sheep can rest and sleep and they can feel secured because they know that their Shepherd is on the scene.

That is why the Lord is MY SHEPHERD! When I am in the presence of the Lord, I feel secured, I can rest, I can sleep comfortably, and I can finally experience a sense of peace that totally surpasses that surpasses all understanding.

When my wife and I first moved to Texas, we stayed in an hotel for three weeks while our newly built home was being completed. There were times when I felt that we had made a huge mistake by moving from Ohio to Texas since we already owned a home in Ohio. I was doubting myself wondering if we should move back to Ohio. One night while sleeping the Lord clearly spoke to me. He said, "I will make a way out of no way." I heard His voice clearly speaking to me. I woke my wife up and told her what the Lord had just said to me. She must have been waiting to hear from the Lord herself because she started crying while she was praying and thanking God. God will speak to you when you call upon Him. What is the Lord speaking to you about today? You will clearly know His voice when He speaks to you because like I said before it is distinguished.

I can understand how it is at times hard to distinguish if this is the Lord speaking or am, I listening to my own conscious. There may be times when the Lord will have to speak the exact same thing over and over before we can get the message. We see one servant in the Bible who God had to call his name several times before he responded.

You remember Samuel from the old testament who was considered to be a judge, a prophet and even a military leader. But, during his younger years, he was called by the Lord. I guess by being young and not being able to clearly recognize the Lord's voice he responded as any young person would. When his name was called, his first response was to the person closest to him, Eli. Then again, the Lord called "Samuel" and Samuel answered, "Here I am" thinking it was Eli. After that third time God called Samuel's name he went to Eli and said, "Here am I."

Eli recognized that it was the lord who was calling him and told Samuel to "lie down: and it shall be, if He call thee, that thou shalt say, Speak, Lord; for thy servant heareth." It should not have to take the Lord to have to speak to you over and over before you hear and understand his voice but sometimes it will.

We hear so many voices, we hear so many people giving us advice, we even pay so called professional people who don't even know us hoping they will give us the best advice in a twenty-minute secession on a situation we have been dealing with for years. How is that? Are you thinking that their decision is better than yours? Are you thinking that because they have years and years of education that they know what is best for you better than you do? God knows what is best for you just try Him!

"God does not yell or scream at you for attention his voice sometimes comes as a whisper:

In the book of Kings (1Kings 19:11 kjv) we find the Lord speaking to Elijah: "Then a great and powerful wind tore the mountains apart and shattered the rocks before the Lord, but the Lord was not in the wind. After the wind there was an earthquake, but the Lord was not in the earthquake. After the earthquake came a fire, but the Lord was not in the fire. And after the fire came a gentle whisper. When Elijah heard it, he pulled his cloak over his face and went out and stood at the mouth of the cave. The Bible says in the next verse (1Kings 19:12 kjv) where Elijah describes the sound of God speaking as "a still small voice."

God knows your situation better than anyone else. He created you, He designed you and He can tell you how to handle any occasion or situation. Nothing is too hard for God. Sometimes you may have to go into a quiet place. You may have to go into a closet, maybe you have to go sit in the car and be alone with God in order to hear from Him.

There have been times when I have been in a crowd or among a group of people and I have heard His voice. Several years ago, we had gotten a letter that offered us a free weekend at a luxurious resort but when we got there it seemed like my wife and I were more or less being forced and intimidated to make a life changing decision at that very moment. We did not know that in order for us to receive the benefits of the resort, we had to listen to this hour-long presentation on buying into a timeshare. After sitting for an hour of listening a guy asked how we wanted to pay for the timeshare either monthly or yearly? Truly, the offer sounded great, we could spend a week at any resort around the world at one very low price and I was almost convinced to give over my credit card. My wife still stood by her answer, "NO."

The salesman walked away and said that my wife and I could talk it over. Here I am finding myself trying to convince my wife to buy into the timeshare when just two hours earlier we both had decided ahead of time that we were not going to buy into it. It took the Lord to step in and speak: "Paul, you cannot afford it, you have more important bills to tend to get up and walk away." After hearing from the Lord my mind was made up and just like that, I got my wife's hand and we got up and walked out. We did get the weeks stay at the resort but, most of all we did not sign anything preventing us from being stuck with a lifelong commitment we more than likely would have regretted later. Sometimes it takes the mighty voice of the Lord to step in to prevent you from involving yourself in things you should not.

It is the upmost importance that if you have not already done so, establish a relationship with Christ so that you are able to hear, recognize and respond to Him in a timely manner. The Lords voice is clear and stands out from anything else.

Prayer:

Dear Lord of Heaven and of Earth, the King of Kings and Lord of Lords, I call upon you now. Father, please forgive me because I know that I have run away from Your love far too long but, now I come to You and I ask you to speak to me in a way that I can hear Your voice clearly and audibly. I need to hear from You Lord right now more than ever! Please speak to me. Come into my heart and fill me with Your love, and I will follow You! I want You to guide me in everything that I do. Please hear my prayers Oh Lord, in the mighty name of Jesus I pray, amen.

Reflection and Chapter Questions

1. Who encouraged you the most during your childhood years?

2. Do you listen to the voices speaking to you during times of decision making?
3. How do you distinguish the voice of the Lord from your own conscious?
4. How much do you value others opinion?
5. How often do you hear from the Lord and He speaks to you?

RSEARCH QUESTION:

Who did God speak to personally in the Bible?
Note: You can find the answer at the end of the book.

CHAPTER 3

HEALTH

"Do you not know that your bodies are temples
of the Holy Spirit, who is in you, whom you have
received from God? You are not your own; you were
brought with a price. Therefore, honor God with
your bodies.

---(1Cor. 6:19-20niv)

It is hard to believe or even think that in a single day one unsuspected
occurrence can alter all your future plans and goals, but I am here
to tell you my dear reader that through all your efforts, as much as
you may try, unexpected occurrences and afflictions can happen. To
be honest, we all pray for the easiest paths to make it through life.
Afflictions can happen to the righteous, the unbeliever, the Minister,
the Deacons, the Priest Everyone. Fact of the matter is, no one is
exempt!

The Bible says in the book of Psalms:

"Many are the afflictions of the
Righteous, But the Lord delivered
him out of them all."

---(Palms 34:19 kjv)

Now, I have a problem with that verse. The words "affliction" and "righteous" are in the same verse! Why would such a loving God, a God of peace and understanding place these two words in the same verse? I think that I would be more able to understand the verse a little better if it said something like:

"Many are the afflictions of the murderers or many are the affliction of the whoremongers or even many are the afflictions of the child molesters."

Then I could of have easily come to the conclusion that they are simply getting what they deserve or what comes around goes around.

But that is not what the bible says.

The Bible says:

"Many are the afflictions of the
Righteous" (psalms 34:19 kjv)

Then if you read a little further in the verse here comes the word BUT. Why was the word BUT put in this verse? That word BUT is a negative conjunction meaning to nullify or to make ineffective. The word BUT negates everything that was previously said. For example:

*Weeping may endure for a night BUT joy cometh in the morning (Psalms 30:5 kjv)

*My days are like a shadow that declineth; and I am withered like grass, BUT, thou O Lord, shalt endure forever; and thy remembrance unto all generations (Psalms 102:11-12 kjv)

After the word "BUT" you find "The Lord delivered them out of them all" and that word ALL means all! Not some of the afflictions, not delivered from a few of the afflictions BUT, the Lord delivered them out of them all!

When I was much younger, I came down with Kidney Failure! Now, let me explain something. The day before I went to the hospital to receive the news, even that same morning I had plans, big plans. I had no idea what was in store for me that day. Even though I knew in my heart that I was not feeling well but as usual, I just thought that I was going through a small trial or maybe a bad cold and that I would soon feel better and get over it. But, not this time.

> "But he said to me, 'My grace is sufficient for you, my power is made perfect in weakness.' Therefore, I will boast all the more gladly about my weaknesses, so that Christ's power may rest on me" (2Corinthians 12:9kjv).

Now my wife Elaina who is in all aspects a true woman of God and one who I trust dearly was always looking out for me. She knew something was going on with me decided to take me to the hospital for a checkup. I, my stubborn self instantly said No! But as caring as my wife was, she never gave up on me and I gave in and got in the car. We went to the hospital, got a few blood tests done and come to find out, my kidneys had failed!

Ok, I can take a few medicines for a while, be back to work at the most in a week or two and I would be feeling better. No, I was all wrong! The doctors tried to explain to everyone who had come to the hospital the process of Hemodialysis. Hemodialysis, what is that? The doctors explained that many dialysis patients needed to get the dialysis treatment for a lifetime or at least until a transplanted kidney would become available but, in the meantime, I had to do dialysis. My heart simply dropped.

That was over thirty-three years ago! Since that time, I have had three kidney transplants, been in a coma, suffered congestive heart failure, double

> The glory of this latter temple shall be greater than the former, say the Lord of host. And in this place, I will give peace, says the Lord of host (Haggai 2:9kjv).

pneumonia, countless surgeries, and let's not forget years and years of sitting in the dialysis chair getting treatment after treatment. I am now living with my fourth transplanted kidney that is working very well! Death was defeated and the grave was denied because God has a purpose and a plan for my life!

> "But the Lord delivered
> them out of them all."
> ---(Palms 34:17kjv)

Even right now as I am writing this book, I am finding myself shedding tears just thinking about that period of my life in 1986! It was a very rough year. Truly my dear reader, we serve a God who has no limits, a God of understanding and one who can heal even the broken hearted. He is our healer and our redeemer!

> Prayer: "I will Praise you Adonai from the rising of the sun till the going down of the same! Father you are my supplier and my protector! How beautiful you are, oh how I need you Jesus! I love you more than life itself. Jesus you are my everything! Please never leave me. I long to see your glorious appearance because you are so beautiful!
> In Jesus name I pray, amen"
>
> Thank You Jesus!

God showed so much grace and mercies towards me so that I could endure. Many days while getting my treatment at the dialysis clinic, I would often feel that my life was over and that my whole purpose of being would be focused around dialysis. But GOD and I will say it again, but GOD had a purpose and a bigger plan for my life!

We are all living in the days of Elijah where walls will come down and will be rebuilt and dry bones will become as flesh. We are also living in the days of Moses where righteousness is being restored! Halleluiah, enemies will be stomped on and the Lord is on the throne and is in control!

> "The glory of this latter temple shall be greater than the former, says the lord of host. And in this place, I will give peace, says the Lord of host."
> ---(Haggai 2:9kjv)

So, why do we especially as Christians have to go through so many trials and suffer at the hands of so many afflictions? I have often thought about that. I try to live right, I pay my tithes, am a faithful member of a Bible teaching church. Hey, I even volunteer in the capacity of a Chaplain at our local hospital on a regular basis talking to patients who are going through and are experiencing similar issues as I have experienced. We often question ourselves as to why our finances are so many times out of balance? Why are our children not living the way I raised them? Why is my body always in so much pain? What do you do when you don't know what to do? You call upon the name of the Lord!

Whatever happened to that happy go lucky upbeat attitude you once had when everything was going exactly right. More than enough money in the bank, children are on the right track, great job, what happened? Why so much suffering in my life? What took away your happiness? We look over our lives and wonder what could we have done differently? We think in what ways could we have treated people differently?

> God said: "Behold, I am the Lord, the God of all flesh. Is there anything too hard for me?
> ---(Jeremiah 32:27 kjv)

Truth is a lot of people simply lack belief that God can do all things! They believe that suffering is just an illusion, that God really does not exist or even that God is limited in his ability. That He wants to help you but is limited by the laws of nature! How ridiculous does that sound?

In this lifetime we will experience circumstances beyond our control. We will experience heartaches and pain, but the Lord says that He will never leave us nor forsake us. He is always with us. But, have you ever just wondered why so many circumstances, why so much pain Lord that you are driven to the point to where you feel that life is not even worth living? My friend, it is because you are experiencing the afflictions of life!

We see in the Bible where even the elite, the very ones who were called by God to fulfill His will were tested and even had to endure afflictions while trying to remain faithful and stay under God's covering.

The illustration of Job seems to me like it is presented during a period of time when the value of a man was not based so much as to how much money they held in the bank but was rather based upon the size of their livestock or how many servants they had.

Job was one who feared God (The beginning of wisdom). Job had it all. In Job's possession was "seven thousand sheep, three thousand camels, five hundred yoke of oxen, five hundred female donkeys and a very large household, so that he was the greatest of all people of the east" (Job 1:3 kjv). Job had it all but, all this changed in the period of just a few days and his faith was tested in the worst way.

We read in the Book of Job that Job was wealthy, upright and was a righteous man. But, in one day it was all taken away from him. We find that one day while satin was going about his daily routine, The Lord saw satin, and this is what took place:

God: "Hey satin, what are you doing?"
Satin: "Oh I'm just going to and fro seeking whom I may devour."
God: "Why don't you pick on someone who will give you a challenge!"

Satin: "Well, who do you got?"

God: "Has thou considered my servant Job?" (Job 1:8 kjv)

Satin: "Yes, Job will meet and exceed the challenges only because you have got that hedge of protection all around him and everything that is dear to him. Job has got the well-fed large livestock, the desired family, bank full of money, Job has got it all but, if you take your hand of protection from him, I guarantee you that Job will curse thee to thy face."

God: "You think that the only reason Job serves me is because of the things that he has? Take it all, I assure you that even without my protective covering over him, he will still be faithful and continue to serve me. Behold, all that he hath is in thy power; only upon himself put forth thine hand" (Job 1:12 kjv). In other words, God gave satin permission to do whatever he wanted to do to Job except this one thing, he could not touch Job's soul.

Now, Job had no idea of the conversation that took place just a few verses earlier between God and satin where satin had to actually get permission from God before he could attack him but all in one day, Job completely lost everything! He lost his family; he lost his finances and even came down with a deadly illness.

After losing everything, even Job's closest friends turned against him, (Eliphaz, Bildad and Zophar).

*Eliphaz's suggestion to Job was that- punishment may be justified or inflicted for secret sins that he had committed (Job 4:7-9kjv).

*Bildad's suggestion to Job was that-infliction and punishment could be the result of something a relative did by accusing his children of sin (Job 8kjv).

*Zophaz stresses to Job to repent of the sins he denies he have committed, so that God can restore his good fortune (11:1 kjv).

I can hear Job's friend's saying things like:

"Man, what did you do? look at you, you got boils all over your body, you have lost your family, lost all your money Job, what did you do?"

But Job simply replied: "I am blameless, I have done absolutely nothing wrong."

Now, I ask you my dear reader while you are going through the most difficult times in your life, your closest friends have turned on you and they have the audacity to question the way you are living or what is going on in your life? I would sincerely question your friendship with them. They finally advised Job to repent and seek God's mercy.

Truly my dear reader even Job seemed to get confused over the entire situation because one-minute Job is saying, "Blessed be the name of the Lord!" And just a little while later Job is cursing the day that he was born." Job was truly being pushed to the limits. One of the few positive things that Job's friends did get right was suggesting to him that a life of faith in Christ Jesus requires us to deal with our sins and to seek and please God.

Finally, after putting Job through so much affliction and suffering and finally realizing that he could not get Job to fall and curse God, satin in his evil plot turns to the one-person closest to Job.

Now, you would think that of all people, that one person who is the closest to you, knows all your habits and private secret thoughts, the one person who has always stood by you that of all people your Wife would be there and stand by your side. Nope, such was not the case for ole Job. Now, down on his luck, sickly, and has lost everything here comes his wife:

"Look at you Job, your body is covered with scales, you got pus oozing out all over your body, our family is gone, we don't have any money, I can't stand to look at you Job, why don't you just curse GOD and die!"

Now Job could have responded to his wife by speaking out of anger, "You did not say that when you were riding around in that nice chariot, you did not say that when you were living in that huge mansion" but Job rebuked her and simply said in return "Thou speaks as one of the foolish women speaketh, shall we receive good at the hand of God and shall not receive evil, naked came I out of my mother's womb, and naketh shall I return thither: The Lord giveth, and the Lord taketh away; blessed be the name of the Lord!" Even his wife could not convince Job to turn his back on God!

"In all this Job sinned not, nor charged God foolishly!"
---(Job 1:22 kjv)

Many times, we as Christians will say things like God gave me this illness but, God does not give His children any type of sickness or ailments. Sickness is of the devil, and he alone should be blamed for it. Believe me when I tell you that when God gives His children things, they are always good things, because He is a good God.

We find in the book of Isaiah that he heard the voice of the Lord, saying "Whom shall I send?" (Isaiah 6:8 kjv). What a powerful question that is, "Whom shall I send?"

NOW, I WANT YOU TO THINK ABOUT SOMETHING
FOR A MOMENT.

HAVE YOU EVER THOUGHT ABOUT WHY
JOB WAS CONSIDERED BY GOD AND NOT
SOME OF THE OTHER SERVANTS?

What about for example His servant Moses?

Yes, Moses indeed he led the people out of Egypt! Moses parted the Red Sea!

But no, God could not consider Moses because, satin would only have to get Moses angry and he will probably end up murdering somebody (Ex. 2:11-12 KJV).

Well what about His servant Noah?

Noah was a righteous man and overcame the flood.

But no, God could not consider Noah because satin would only have to put an alcoholic drink in front of Noah, and he will probably show up intoxicated (Gen. 9:20-21 KJV).

Now, here is a dedicated servant, what about David?

Yes David, now this is a man after God's own heart! David was a great fighter and known as the "sweet psalmist of Israel" (2 Sam 23:1kjv). David also was the author and source of poems and songs.

But no, God could not consider David because satin would only have to put a beautiful woman in front of David and David will absolutely lose his mind thinking about that Sheba (2 Sam. 12:24 KJV).

Oh, I got it! Solomon:

Now this was a man who was different from all the previous servants of GOD and you would have thought that King Solomon would have been the Lord's first choice!

Yes, Solomon was indeed not only considered to be the wisest man that ever lived but also had power beyond either of the previous kings of the country!

But no, God could not even consider Solomon because even though he did love many women as his Father did Solomon was different. Solomon loved strange woman! Solomon loved strange women from many different tribes: The Moabites, The Ammonites, The Edomites, The Zidonnians, The Hittites and even the daughter of Pharaoh and Solomon would easily be distracted (1 Kings 11:1 KJV).

GOD could not recommend or consider just anybody for satins challenges.

I ask you my dear reader, do you feel that God has enough faith in you that He would consider you to face the harsher challenges of life? Do you really feel that you are not only physically strong enough but also mentally and spiritually strong enough to overcome them and after all was over still serve God faithfully?

Have you ever questioned yourself as to why am I always going through what seems like the very same trials year after year? Why do I have to suffer so much pain? Why Me? Truly, my dear reader the answer can usually be found in the way you respond.

How will you respond when finances fail you?

How will you respond when sickness comes upon you?

How will you respond when facing temptation?

> "The righteous cry out, and the Lord hears, and delivers them out of all their troubles. The Lord is near to those who have a broken heart and saves such as have a contrite spirit."
>
> ---(Psalms 34:17-18 kjv)

We can clearly see in this passage and learn of God's compassion and grace in the way God restored Job's fortune. Even through his toughest trials, he never gave up faith in God. Job relied on God. My dear reader, you can try to fight with all your might, you can spend your last dime on people who try to help you but truly the time is now that we need to repent of our sins and get in line and in touch with the Holy Spirit. God hears your cries. When you pray, you activate the Will of God. He hears your prayers and He is here willing and able to come through for you each and every time.

Prayer:

Dear Heavenly Father, I am ready for a change in my life. My body is in so much pain and the medicines are not working anymore. I have suffered from health issues for such a very long time and I can't hardly take it anymore. I know that you have a plan for my life that does not include pain and I am ready to step into the purpose you have set for me. Truly, I am tired. My body is tired, my mind is tired I need You to heal me Lord. I am willing to wait for You to do a work in my life and it does not matter how long it takes. If it takes an entire lifetime, I don't mind waiting on You Lord! Please hear my prayer!

In Jesus name I pray, Amen.

Reflection and Chapter Questions

1. What circumstances have you ever experienced in life that has affected your health?
2. How can you model Job's response to life's challenges in your own life?
3. Who is your biggest comforter during times of serious health crisis?

4. What is your belief when it comes to doctor's healing and the healing that God provides?
5. In what ways do you feel that God was trying or testing your faith?

RESEARCH QUESTION:

How was Job losing7000 sheep detrimental to his burnt offerings?
Note: You can find the answer at the end of the book

CHAPTER 4

A CONFUSED MIND

Oh, you of little faith, why did you doubt?
---(Matthew 14:31 esv)

A confused mind is a doubtful and an unbelieving mind. When we talk about doubt and unbelieving, we can easily interchange the two and put them in the same sentence usually meaning the same thing but, in all aspect, they are completely different in so many ways as well.

I love to read the book of James, especially the first chapter. That very first chapter gives a very good or even excellent scriptures that describes and helps us to understand on how to overcome confusion and how we can receive what we need from God. If you ask me, a man who is always doubtful and has a confused mind is simply double-minded. In my bible which is the King James Version, it gives a clear example of confusion as one goes back and forth, back, and forth, never being able to decide on anything. As soon as he thinks he has made a clear choice, here comes doubt, confusion and unbelief causing him to have two minds once again. He is uncertain about everything and sometimes even doubting himself.

We find the Greek meaning of the word <u>Doubtful</u> is *"apeitheia"* and is defined in the verb form as:

> ... to waver, to hesitate. Consider questionable or
> unlikely; hesitate to believe to distrust.

We find the Greek meaning of the word
<u>Unbelief</u> is "Apistia" and is defined in the noun form as:

> *...unfaithfulness, faultless*

Doubt

Several years ago, while I was working in the capacity as a Chaplain at the local hospital, (well, I still work there) I came across a young man around the age of thirty who was dealing with a serious problem. He was debating whether or not he should have a major surgery.

> "How long halt ye between two opinions?"
> ---(1 Kings 18:21 kjv)

When I entered the young man's room, I found him sitting on the side of the bed with his head in his Bible and a huge frown on his face. He was reading healing scriptures and confessing the Word of GOD over his body. At the same time, he was being attacked by spirits of doubt.

As we began to talk, he explained that he badly needed to have an immediate surgery to his spinal cord that would heal several bones in his body which in turn would relieve the excruciating pain he had been suffering from for a very long time. This pain prevented him from working, sleeping, and basically living a normal life.

But, at the same time he felt doubtful and fearful because he knew people who had gotten the same surgery performed on them before and came out feeling even worse than before they had the surgery done and could barely stand or walk afterwards. He was completely confused as to what to do.

"Verily, verily, I say unto thee, when thou wast young, thou girdest thyself, and walkedst whither thou wouldest: but when thou shall be old, thou shalt stretch forth thy hands, and another shall gird thee, and carry thee whither thou wouldest not."

---(John 21:18 kjv)

What do you do when you don't know what to do? You call upon the name of the Lord! We prayed for a while and the young man gave me a surprised look as if he had just been woken up to a new day. After we prayed, he explained that he had been going through a rough time in life dealing with school, parents, friends and even church which had made it even difficult to pray at times. Every time he started to pray for guidance, thoughts of him after the surgery of not being able to walk, not being able to stand upright and having more pain would cross his mind. I said to the young man, "Let's pray again." I sat on the side of the bed and we began to pray but this time we prayed out loud. After we prayed a second time the young man said that while we were praying God spoke to him and he saw a vision. This time GOD opened his mind and eyes to the Spirit world.

This is the vision he saw:

Demons were feeding him lies. First, that he would not be healed and secondly, that reading healing scriptures was a waste of time. But each time he confessed by mouth the Word of GOD, streams of fire would come out of his mouth and the demons would scatter and flee!

Being in the spirit world GOD showed the young man that he had much faith and that was the reason as to why demons were attacking him by having a doubtful mind. Doubts will come in the form of imaginary thoughts we entertain that are contrary to the Word of GOD. Saints believe me when I tell you that having a doubtful mind is not something GOD puts in us. God does not even want the word "Doubt" to be in our vocabulary.

"Trust in the Lord with all thine heart; and lean not unto thine own understanding. In all thy ways acknowledge him, and He shall direct thy paths. Be not wise in thine own eyes: fear the lord and depart from evil. It shall be health to thy navel, and marrow to thy bones" (Proverbs 3:5-8 kjv).

The young man was able to overcome having a mind full of doubt and eventually had the surgery done. He now attends a State University and is a respected member of the school and its school's Track team. I ask you "Is there anything too hard for God?"

I truly believe that Jesus bores all of our sins and that He will deliver us and make us free from having a doubtful and confused mind. One being doubtful is one who is not completely able to make decisive decisions on important matters. It comes to mind the man at The Pool of Bethesda who was desperately seeking

> "And by him all that believe are justified from all things, from which ye could not be justified by the law of Moses."
> Acts 13:39(KJV)

and desiring to be healed from infirmities he had been suffering from for thirty-eight very long years. When Jesus saw him, He said to him, *"Do you want to be made well?"* But there was a difficulty in the way.

The man had one eye on the pool and one eye on Jesus. I see that even today; many people are getting cross-eyed and confused in the exact same way. Just like the man we talked about earlier who was debating whether if he should get the well needed surgery or not. The problem with the man at The Pool of Bethesda was that he was confused as to where his healing was going to come from. He had one eye on the doctors and medicines and one eye on Jesus.

If you will only look to Christ and put both of your eyes on Him, every bit of your life can be made whole— body, spirit, and soul. It is mentioned in the book of (Acts 13:39 kjv), where it is the promise of God that those who "believe are justified (*made free or innocent*) from all things."

Unbelief

Many years ago, my wife, I, and our children were living in a two-bedroom apartment. We had been living there for almost ten years. During that time, we were both working and still things were hard for us. Even though we paid all of our bills on time but by the middle of the month we only had a few dollars left to spend

> Ask what you desire and it shall be done. (John 15:7 kjv)

on ourselves. One night my wife Elaina had a dream that we were going to buy a house. Not just any house, but a brand new one built from the ground up. The next morning, we sat in the bed and I listened as she explained to me her dream. She went into great detail the room sizes, carpet color and even down to the faucet styles. After the dream to my surprise Elaina began to start buying items for a house that we did not have. She would buy new silverware, curtains and rods, new bedspreads. She even brought a brand-new couch which did not fit in our two- bedroom apartment, so we had to store a lot of items in her Mom's extra room. But, when Elaina brought a full-size pool table, I felt that she was going overboard. My Mom agreed to allow us to keep the pool table in her upstairs bedroom. We had stuff in people's homes all around the city. I always wanted to keep my wife happy and pleased but truly I did not think that we would ever be in the position to buy a house since we were struggling just living in an apartment.

Just to be on the safe side and give me a peace of mind I told Elaina to keep all the receipts for everything that she was buying because in the back of my mind I felt that we were going to return everything back to the stores where all this stuff came from when all this was over.

My wife Elaina has always been known by many believers and friends as having a Joseph spirit within her. Now, if you remember

33

Joseph in the Bible, he was the one who was considered to be a dreamer. He would dream things and they would come to pass. In Joseph's first dream, he dreamed:

"For behold, we were binding sheaves in the field, and, lo, my sheaf arose, and also stood upright; and, behold, your sheaves stood round about, and made obeisance to my sheaf" (Gen.37:7 kjv).

In his second dream, Joseph dreamed:

"Behold, I have dreamed a dream more; and, behold, the sun and the moon and the eleven stars made obeisance to me" (representing his father, mother and eleven brothers) were bowing down to him. In the end, Joseph's dreams did come true and he became second in command over the entire land of Egypt and everyone was required to bow down to him including his family when they were in his presence.

> "And without faith it is impossible to please God, because anyone who comes to him must believe that he exists and that he rewards those who earnestly seek him."
>
> ---(HEBREWS 11:6 kjv)

Like I mentioned before, my wife having a Joseph spirit at heart went on with every check she got from work she would buy a little something for what I called our imaginary house. Believe it or not over time we had purchased everything needed to fill a brand-new house only thing though, we did not have a house. That is what I mean when people say that my wife has a Joseph spirit.

> "Truly I tell you, whoever says to this mountain, be lifted up and thrown into the sea! And does not doubt at all in his heart but that what he says will take place, it will be done for him. For this reason, I am telling you, whatever you ask for in prayer, believe

34

(trust and be confident) that it is granted to you, and
you will (get it).

---*(Mark 11:23-24 amp)*

One day out of nowhere we received through the mail a flyer
from a builder who was building new houses in the area especially
for new home buyers! I thought to myself "NO WAY, this cannot
be real." When Elaina got home from work, I showed her the flyer
and she called the builder. He came to our apartment and explained
everything we needed to do in order for us to get approved for a
loan before the building process could begin. Family members did
not believe in us. Close friends did not believe in us but, we believed
in GOD!

Once we got approved for the lot through City Council and
the loan, I began to come around and I started to believe that this
crazy idea of my wife just might be possible. Every day I would ride
up to this empty lot full of trees and bushes and I would stare and
imagine what a house would look like being built there. A garage on
the left side, kids playing in this huge backyard. Yard lights and an
exceptionally long driveway.

Every time my wife and I would bring up the issue of us buying
a house to people many would respond by saying "Are yall still on
that house buying thing, why don't you two just stop talking about
it, give it up, it is never going to happen!"

"Jesus said unto him, if thou canst believe, all
things are possible to him that believeth."
--- (Mark 9:23-25 kjv)

But, one day, about 6am in the morning and still dark outside,
I was at the lot starring at it as usual and Lord and behold coming
around the corner would you believe it?

A Big Yellow Bull Dozer!

I looked and I looked and I thought to myself, "Is this for real, Is this thing coming to our lot?" The bulldozer got closer and closer, so I pulled my car out of the way just in case. Several cars followed and men wearing white hats got out the cars. They pulled out many blueprints and laid them across the hood of the cars and occasionally looked over to the lot pointing to it. I called Elaina who was home still sleep and I yelled "Elaina they are here, they are getting ready to start digging, they brought bulldozers' and everything, you got to get up here!" Elaina slowly replied, "Ok, call me if they need me" and she went back to sleep. I thought maybe she did not hear me. The builders built our new home exactly the way we had planned and it was beautiful!

The builder finished building our brand-new home in just over four months. When all was completed the builder finally called us one night around seven. He said, "Mister and Misses Phillips, your new home is completely finished. You can move into your new home the first thing in the morning." Being totally excited, I tried to remain as calm as possible as I replied, "Sir, is it possible if we can start moving into our home right now?"

I could tell from the builder's voice over the phone that he had a huge smile on his face as he replied, "Of course you can, I am still here at the new home sight and if you come now you can pick up the keys."

Elaina streamed, "Halleluiah, thank you Jesus!" We woke up our three daughters, grabbed our coats and speedily drove towards our new home! Elaina and I were praying, thanking God out loud and crying all at the same time. We now had a brand-newly built

> Now unto him that is able to do exceedingly abundantly above all that we ask or think, according to the power that worketh in us. Eph. 3:20(KJV)

home and since Elaina had previously brought everything we needed, within two weeks the house was fully furnished and it looked like a showroom exhibit. Yes, I must admit that at times I was full of doubt. Not believing in us buying a home, Not believing in my wife and overall, not believing that GOD would do this for us.

> "Behold I am the Lord the God of all flesh is there anything too hard for me?"
>
> ---(JEREMIAH 32:27 kjv)

Having a doubtful mind and an unbelieving heart can not only be a time-consuming effort but can also make a situation even dangerous. We must continually put our trust in God knowing that He is willing and able to do anything exceedingly and abundantly above all that we ask for or think, according to the power that worketh in us. It is never too late to dream, but always be careful who you share your dreams and hopes with because a lot of people will try to destroy your dreams. The very things that you have dreamed and prayed on for years, believe me there are people praying against you for your hopes and dreams to not come to pass.

No one has the authority or power to shatter or destroy your dreams unless you allow them to do so. Sometimes it may be necessary to keep your hopes, dreams and ambitions between you and The Lord!

Prayer:

Dear Lord, I need Your help. Right now, I'm dealing with so many different issues and my life at times has become so overwhelming. I feel so lost and confused and many times I don't know whether I'm coming or going. I feel hopeless and so lost deep down inside. I need You Lord to step in and take control over my life and cleanse me and refresh my mind. Give me a pure heart and a mind of understanding. I love You Lord; I praise and I worship You and I give You all of the honor. In Jesus precious name I pray, Amen.

Reflection and Chapter Questions

1. What issues do you most likely have doubt about in making decisions?
2. What scriptures do you find most helpful and turn to when you find yourself being unsure about things?
3. How much do you value the opinion of others?
4. In what ways can you incorporate God's wisdom and direction at a greater level in your own personal decisions and planning?
5. Has there ever been a time in your life when a dream has helped or affected you in making choices and decisions?

RESEARCH QUESTION:

In this section, Paul talks about Joseph. Why was Joseph so despised by his brothers?

Note: You can find the answer at the end of the book

CHAPTER 5

OVERCOMING TEMPTATION

Watch and pray, that ye enter not into temptation:
the spirit is willing, but the flesh is weak
---(Matthew 26:41 kjv)

Have you ever tried to simplify or define the word temptation? Generally speaking, temptation is having an urge or being enticed to do or say something wrong. Now, temptation and sin are not the same thing because it is not a sin to be tempted but it is a sin to give into temptation! We are tempted every day to say or do things that are ungodly but when you cross the line and say inappropriate things it constitutes sinful slander.

One of the greatest temptations we face is being impulsive. When you decide to do or act upon a situation now without giving thought, reasonable reason for doing it you are acting upon impulse. For example: You go to the grocery store with the intent on buying only a few groceries. You happen to walk pass the women's dept. and see a dress that you just must have. This dress is nothing like the fifty dresses in your closet and you must have it. Without any thought on price, if you really need another dress you toss it in the cart. That is acting upon impulse and can be overcome through prayers. Before making a final decision on a major issue, I have listed four things to consider first:

1. Get all the facts: What was your initial intent?
2. Set aside time: Set aside time to think it over.
3. Look over all options: If you decide to do it, will your decision prevent you from doing something else?
4. Pray: What do you do when you don't know what to do? You call upon the name of the Lord! When you pray before making impulsive or indecisive choices and decisions, God will provide you with spiritual wisdom and spiritual answers.

Have you ever been tempted to really speak your mind, or you felt that you needed to bite your tongue to keep you from saying what was really on your mind? The first way to overcome temptation is to identify it. If you have a problem with alcoholism, you may have to stop going into alcoholic establishments like bars or places where they serve alcohol. If you

> Blessed is the man that endures temptation: for when he is tried, he shall receive the crown of life which the Lord has promised to them who love Him (James 1:12 kjv).

have a problem with drug abuse, you may have to avoid people who are doing drugs. Think about this, what is the one thing that you struggle with the most? Do you have and urge or are you tempted to speed while driving? Are you tempted to be around a certain group of people who you know are no good for you? Be honest with yourself and say "God, I have a problem with _____ and I need help" and God will help you. Temptation is a deadly spirit and we must try to control it. You can become a slave to what controls you or what you fall into temptation to. We are tempted to eat too much, tempted to go places you should not go, tempted to watch things that are not appropriate. God created you to be free. You need a change of mind and a change of heart in order to truly be free.

"But every man is tempted, when he is drawn away of his own lust, and enticed. Then when lust hath conceived, it bringeth forth sin: and sin, when it is finished, bringeth forth death"

(James1:14-15 kjv).

The sin has been committed when you overindulge yourself with food. When you enter an establishment that is ungodly. When you allow your eyes

"Resist the devil, and he will flee from you. Draw nigh to God, and he will draw nigh to you" (James 4:7-8 kjv).

to watch inappropriate television shows, you have crossed the line and it is no longer a temptation but because you acted upon it, it has become a sin. Everyone has their own struggles and battles when it comes to temptation. If you think about it, usually it is the small things that keep you trapped from fulfilling God's purpose for you. Tempted to hoard money, keeps you from tithing properly. Tempted to sleep more keeps you from doing what really needs to be done today but you have put off until tomorrow.

One of the reasons so many suffer from the same temptation year after year is because they simply refuse to ask God for help. You have to pray so that your spirit man will become stronger than your inner man! When you get up in the morning ask God to give you strength to resist temptation. The worst lie you could ever say to yourself is "Just one more cigarette and I am done, or just one more alcoholic drink and I am going to quit." You are still an alcoholic when you have a bottle of alcohol in your hand. You are fooling yourself thinking that you can stop smoking at any time when you have a cigarette in your mouth and a pack in your pocket, you are just in denial. Turn your life around and pray and ask God for help! He will help you, but you have to make that first step by calling upon Him! Temptation is everywhere and can happen to anyone.

We read in the book of Genesis (39:1-20 kjv) where Potiphar's wife who was known for her infidelities took a liking to Joseph and tried to seduce him. When Joseph refused her advance's, he ran off but she retaliated by falsely accusing Joseph of trying to rape her, and Potiphar had Joseph thrown in prison. Even when the temptation looks good and pleasing, sometimes you may have to tighten up your shoestrings and run away from it in order to prevent yourself from falling into it. It's ok to run away from a situation rather than be caught or trapped into it. When you identify your weakness, God will give you strength to overcome it.

Suggestions:

* * Don't put yourself in the position to be tempted!
* * You may have to change friends or associates!
* * Don't ever compromise your integrity
* * Always be honest with yourself

There is a temporary pleasure in giving into temptation, but in the long run it will catch up to you! Drugs may feel good at the present time but what is it doing to your mind and your way of thinking? You are married and you are having an affair on your spouse? It may feel good and it may even seem right at the present time but what effect will it have on your marriage in the long run and not to mention the mental state of the children once they find out?

One of the first keys to resisting temptation is knowing that Satan is behind all of that and he is the supreme "tempter" (Matthew 4:3 kjv). Satin has been tempting mankind since God placed Adam and Eve in the garden of Eden (Gen. 3:1 kjv). Another key to resisting temptation is being consistently obedient. Let me give you a few examples. If you constantly are obedient to resist the urge to have a cigarette, over time you will get stronger and not even have the desire for it. If you are constantly obedient in avoiding having an alcoholic drink over time you will lose the taste of it. You have to constantly be obedient in resisting temptations in order to overcome it as well. You may feel that you have overcome a specific temptation but, the problem occurs when you begin to tolerate other's behavior. For example, you have just overcome drug abuse but you tolerate it and are ok with people doing it around you. Actually, there should be no compromise at all and you should remove yourself from their company! You have to take a stance with love that there is a line that you will not cross and you have to set a standard and that standard is God!

Temporary pleasure is never a good thing and only leads to heartache and discontent! You have recognize and identify your problem, then you must ask God for help to strengthen your inner spirit to resist temptation. Only then are you on your way to fulfilling God's purpose He has set for you!

Reflection and Chapter Questions

1. What has been your greatest temptation in your life?
2. In what ways can you pray more effectively struggling with temptation?
3. Which Bible verse gives us God's wonderful promise concerning temptation?
4. What is your definition of "Fleeing from temptation?"
5. How did Jesus respond to temptation?

Research Question

If God doesn't tempt us, why do you think that the Lord's prayer petition Him not to lead us into temptation?

Note: You can find the answer at the end of the book

CHAPTER 6

SINS OF THE TONGUE

"Death and life are in the power of the tongue:
and they that love it shall eat the fruit thereof."
---(Proverbs 18:21 kjv)

The Greek word for *"tongue"* is *"glossa"* meaning to speak, talk, chat, pattle or to make sound. The Bible describes the tongue this way: "The tongue is a fire, a world of evil among the parts of the body. It corrupts the whole body, sets the whole course of one's life on fire, and is itself set on fire by hell" (James 3:9-12 kjv).

When I was younger growing up in a small town located in the southern part of Cincinnati, I would often hear my mom say things like "watch your mouth", or "your mouth is going to get you in a lot of trouble." Usually that would come after I would say something totally out of context. When she said that she was going to wash my mouth out with a bar of soap I was actually afraid to even look at soap thinking of the taste being in my mouth. My usual response would be "Mom, I did not mean to say that." Why is it that just a few simple words out of your mouth can cause so much trouble? The words we speak out of our mouth can be deadly and sometimes life altering to someone else.

Things such as Gossiping, spreading rumors, slandering someone's reputation, or reviling your remarks with abusive language. The tongue can do so much harm if we allow it to do so by not controlling how we speak to each other.

The Bible says that "Death and life are in the power of the tongue" (Proverbs 18:21 kjv).

When my three daughters were growing up, I would often say to them "Be careful how you talk to people. You can say the exact same words to someone and the way you say it will be a deciding factor as to how they will receive it."

Let me give you an example:

You have heard someone say, "I can't stand you." The way they express the statement actually determined how a person was going to receive it. They can say "I cannot stand you" with a frown and squinted eyes and a person will more than likely take it seriously and probably get hurt from the person saying it. On the other hand, a person can say the exact same words "I can't stand you" with a smile and a giggle and the receiving person will not take it so seriously and will probably laugh along with the person saying it. They spoke the exact same words, but their presentation was different and the person who they said it to, took it totally different. It was all about their presentation.

Regardless, we should always be mindful of the way we treat and speak to people. All of us have feelings and some of us are more sensitive than others. God tells us in His Word that the tongue has incredible power "that we praise our Lord and the Father, and with it we curse men, who have been made in God's likeness" (James 3 kjv).

You can either bring a blessing to someone or a curse and death to someone based on your words. Believe it or not we can speak life or death over a person. There was a time when I was playing little league basketball for our

> The mouth of the just bringeth wisdom: but the forward tongue shall be cut out. The lips of the righteous know what is acceptable: but the mouth of the wicked speaketh forwardness (Proverbs 10:31-32 kjv).

community. The team was already having a losing season and many people were beginning to wonder why that year after year the team had a losing season. We had very good players, nice uniforms and even a huge gym to workout in. So why did we so often have a losing season? One day while we were practicing one of the parents came to watch us work out. He sat on a bench and noticed that the coach was saying things like: You guys are not as good as some of the other teams I have seen, you all will never be able to play high school ball if you keep playing the way you do." The players had developed the mindset that they were not good enough and would never amount to anything. Even the far and in between small positive remarks were spoken in a negative manner. Our team was never meant to be successful all because the coach never spoke winning words into our lives. He was soon removed. The next year we were given a new coach who gave only positive reinforcement and for the next couple of years we only lost one game. The words that come out of our mouth can be life threatening and leave lifelong damage in us, especially when it comes to the children. Many times, we need to pray before we speak instead of just saying the first thing to come to your mind. We can overcome the tongue when we pray and think things over first. My wife was particularly good at that especially when it came time to disciplining our children. When a child would misbehave, my wife would sometimes be angry but would always pray before giving a spanking. She would sit a daughter of ours down and explain to them what they did and that she prayed on how many spankings they were to receive.

One time I will not mention which one asked their Mom if she could pray again to see if the Lord had lowered the amount of spankings they were going to receive. We put a lot of emphasizes on the tongue I guess it is because the tongue is what presents information to us. The tongue is considered evil and full of deceit and is no way being able to control it. Just maybe we need to practice silence if we cannot control what comes out of our mouth.

The Bible gives us a very good example where someone had spoken something and later had to regrettably stand by what they had said. We see were King Herod on his birthday was entertaining guest and his niece Salome the daughter of Herodias and Herod11 came to dance before them. King Herod promised in front of everyone to give his niece whatever she would ask (Matt.14:7 kjv).

I guess King Herod was perhaps thinking that she may ask for something like more servants, a huge mansion, or a fleet of chariots, but what she asked for totally surprised King Herod. Being advised beforehand by her mother Herodias as what to say to King Herod, Herodias daughter (Salome) said, "Give me here John Baptist's head in a charger" (Matt. 14:8 kjv).

Because King Herod had spoken in the midst of guest, he was expected to fulfil his nieces wish. John the Baptist was beheaded in prison and his head was delivered in a charger as Salome had requested.

We must be careful what comes out of our mouths. Our words could mean

> Death and life are in the power of the tongue: and they that love it shall eat the fruit (Proverb 18:21 kjv.)

life or death in situations. We must control the tongue because it can at times lead us into doing things, we later will regret but God can help us with this.

> "For this God is our God for ever: He will be our guide even unto death" (Psalms 48:14 kjv).

When we pray in the spirit and are under the power of God's anointing the Holy Spirit will go before us and guide us on what to say, how we should present it and the appropriate time we should speak on certain things.

Reflection and Chapter Questions

1. In what situations have your tongue gotten you into trouble?

2. Do you use facial or hand gestures when expressing yourself?

3. Who in your life have you found to always speak negatively on all issues?

4. How can you control how you speak whether it be positive or negative?

5. How has the Holy Spirit helped you in what and how you will present your speech or words?

RSEARCH QUESTION:

What was the main reason as to why Herodias daughter (Salome) asked for the head of John The Baptist?

Note: You can find the answer at the end of the book

CHAPTER 7

OVERCOMING LONELINESS

"…and there is a friend that sticketh closer than a brother."
---(PROVERBS 18:24 kjv)

Mother Theresa once said that the most common disease in this world is not cancer or AIDS or heart disease. She said that the most common disease was simply loneliness!

I grew up in a family of nine people including my parents. The house was always noisy, crowded and someone was always arguing with someone else. To say that our house was always busy is an understatement. There was always something going on. We as a family were always going on trips, reunions, fishing outings and so on. Seems like there was never a time of rest. Living at home, I do not remember a time that I could consider myself as being lonely.

Truly, I believe that the first time in my life that I actually experienced loneliness was when I first got into college. Weeks before leaving for college, I was excited and could not wait to leave home. But, that first day on the campus, as I watched my family drive away without me, for the first time in my entire life I experienced the feeling of being completely alone and isolated.

We find in the Holy Bible the Prophet Jeremiah who was considered by many scholars as being "the weeping prophet" because of the often-gloomy nature of his message and the grief he expressed for his people. The prophet Jeremiah not only suffered from rejection by the very ones he loved But he also experienced much loneliness throughout his life.

Jeremiah was called to preach by God, but God forbid him from marrying, and to not have any children. He lived alone, he ministered alone, was rejected and was really poor. Jeremiah was experiencing the spirit of loneliness. But, even after much suffering, Jeremiah showed great strength and spiritual faith. Even though he suffered a great sense of failure and a lot of despair in his life, Jeremiah had a deep relationship with God and promised God that he would bring Judah and Israel back from captivity and would rebuild them as they were before (Jere. 33:7 kjv).

"Cursed be the day wherein I was born: let the day wherein my mother bare me blessed." (Jeremiah 20:14 kjv)

Everyone at one time or another will have struggled with some form of loneliness. I am sure that there have been times in your life when you have been lonely or you just simply needed someone or something to talk to, even if it was talking to that fluffy cat sitting on your beautiful couch, it did not matter who or what it was (no I am kidding about the cat). Someone who would simply take the time to listen to you without any interruptions. One who would understand you and accepts you just the way you are. I am telling you, that is what a real friend does, and they are very rare to find.

When true friends become hard to find we often find ourselves disconnecting ourselves from others or connecting with the wrong people or crowd. When we begin to finally separate those who are true and dear to us from those who are false and hide their real identity behind a smile or handshake, we often find ourselves experiencing one of the many facets of life and that is *loneliness*.

Now, many people feel that being alone and experiencing

loneliness are practically the same thing but, they are quite different in many ways. Unlike being *alone,* loneliness often applies that you may be looking for something or someone to feel complete. While on the other hand, being alone allows you to give yourself the freedom to be introspective, time to think for yourself and possibly allow you to make better decisions and choices without being impacted by outside influences.

Loneliness can in many ways be compared to what one experience by being incarcerated or confined to specific areas for extensive periods of time. If you think about it, a person in jail experience such things as being alone, being separated, being estranged, and basically living in isolation.

Can you imagine having everything in life you ever imagined? Imagine that money was no object, you had garages full of expensive vehicles and you could build multiple mansions of any dimension or size. You were so wealthy that all you had to do was point to an object not even considering the cost and it was paid for in full but after all this good fortune, you had no one to share it with. I think that I would lay in the bed of one of those huge beautiful mansions all by myself feeling completely miserable and lonely. Your happiness is based on your feelings and comes with a price, but your joy comes from pure facts. Money can give you temporary happiness, but your real joy comes from the fact in knowing that The Lord is your provider of all your needs and that the Lord has already written out your life's plan.

I once had a classmate who graduated with me from High School. Over the years we had kept in touch through social media. Often, we would share with each other the things that were going on in each other's life. He was divorced and had one son. Me, I was married with three daughters a cat, a dog, and a bird. He would often tell me how happy he was after the divorce living with his son. He had a great job, good friends and living in a very nice neighborhood. My life on the other hand was what you would probably consider as the simple life. But, year after year I would listen to him as he would put into words how much joy he had in his life until one day it all changed.

It was around three in the morning when I got a call from him crying uncontrollably over the phone. He was trying to tell me that his only son had just been killed in a car accident. I tried to console him, but I do not think that he was hearing me. He kept saying "My son is gone, my son is gone." I just kept quiet with my ears open. After about an hour or two, he began to calm down a little. We talked until he eventually fell asleep on the phone. The next day, I called him to see if he was ok and how he was doing. His place was full of people and I could barely hear him speak. Sad to say, I could tell by his voice that his body was weak from crying and grieving all night. He went into another room so we could talk. He explained to me what had happened to his son and it brought tears to my eyes. Weeks later after all was over, I got a call from him. The once happy go lucky person that I once knew was gone. He told me that his home now feels empty, there is no joy in his life and that he really feels like he has nothing to live for anymore.

I tried to console him but once again, painful heartache had over taken him. He asked me "Paul, when will this feeling of grief and despair ever end?"

My answer, "Truly my friend, a lot of times when we go through tough moments of misery and suffer through distressful periods throughout life those feelings of grief and despair we feel sometimes never end." Being alone especially over long periods of time is a serious issue and

> And the Lord said, it is not good that the man should be alone, I will make him an help meet for him (Gen. 2:18 kjv).

can affect our mental stability. We often realize and find that you were simply talking to yourself. We find ourselves crying for no particular reason. God did not create or intend for anyone to be alone. Loneliness is real. The solution and the best way to overcome this spirit of loneliness is with GOD!

Loneliness can be categorized into two conditions or areas:

1. Situational loneliness

   These are areas of experiencing loneliness where you have no control over such as the times when you were ill. You may have had to go to the hospital for weeks with no visitors and once finally released and you are at home, the same thing happens. No calls or visitors and it seems like no one cares. Situational loneliness can also occur for example let us say you had to move into a totally new area or even worse than that a different state where for weeks and months at a time you did not know a single person. Once again, no calls or visitors and you feel no one is even thinking about you or even cares.

2. Emotional loneliness

   These are areas of loneliness where you for example you have many friends. You can call on them, discuss life issues and problems but suddenly you call for prayer and they let you down. You may mention that you are low on money and the rent is due. Their response is "I will pray on it." You about to get kicked out of your home and their response, "I will pray on it." Watch out for people like that. You are looking for more, but your so-called friends of many years have let you down. Your mind is left with feelings of depression, loneliness, let down and basically forsaken. You must find a way to protect your emotions, so you will not end up feeling lonely

I am here to tell you my dear reader you are never forsaken, and you are never alone. Jesus died on the cross so that we would never be alone. No matter the situation or what you may have done in your life, Jesus still loves you just as much as when you committed sin and you failed Him as when you were totally faithful and you were committed to Him. When you have a relationship with Christ your sins are forgiven, and you are never alone.

You may be going through some of the most difficult struggles of your life and people just can't figure you out or understand why you are still crying out and thanking the Lord so much. They really don't understand that when you are supposed to be miserable and down how you can still praise and worship and dance for the Lord uncontrollably so much. People don't understand why you are always on your knees praying so hard all the time. Maybe it is because they just don't know or have a clue as to what you have been going through these past several months!

Maybe they don't completely understand the pain you are suffering or how you are one check away from losing everything you have worked your entire life for, but through the grace of God, The Lord brought you through! Yes, you have a huge reason to shout and scream! Yes, you have a reason to worship like never before! Yes indeed, you have many reasons to holler and praise the Lord for His goodness, that's why!

In life we will undoubtably experience unexpected misery but, The Bible says:

> …. "let not your heart be troubled; ye believe in God, believe also in me. In my Father's house are many mansions; if it were not so, I would have told you. I go to prepare a place for you, I will come again and receive you to myself; that where I am, there you may be also." (JOHN 14:1-3 KJV)

Remember that one of the most important things in life is to Love God, to love others and to love Yourself! That is why it is essential to continually keep your mind focused on Christ and not let anything or anyone come in between the love you have for Him.

Reflection and Chapter Questions

1. At what times do you feel most lonely?
2. How has being alone affected you mentally?
3. Is there a certain person in your life you can call upon when the feeling of loneliness comes upon you?
4. How do you help others battling loneliness?
5. What really helped you to overcome the spirit of loneliness?

RESERCH QUESTION:

What is the main reason as to why God did not allow Jeremiah to marry?

Note: You can find the answer at the end of the book

CHAPTER 8

VICTORY OVER DEPRESSION

Humble yourself, therefore, under God's mighty hand, that he may lift you up in due time. Cast all your anxiety on him because he cares for you.

--- (1 Peter 5:6-7 kjv)

When I lost my Father in 2014, people were wondering if I was even sad, depressed or down trotted because of the way I was responding to the loss of my father because outwardly, I was not showing any signs of a person bereaving. I was smiling, shaking hands, hugging but on the inside my heart and body was being ripped apart. My Father in law (rest his soul) actually had to say to me "Paul, you don't have to keep standing up shaking hands and sitting down with everyone that walks past." He knew that my body was weak. The sad thing about it is that I did not even realize that my mind and body was actually grieving in its own way.

The thing is, the human brain is awesomely designed by God. My mind had fixed itself in a way so that my feelings would be able to handle the death of my father and I would not have a total breakdown. Even though, I felt normal, my body was responding totally different. Getting out of the limousine at the grave site my legs suddenly just gave out and I fell to the ground. I looked up still wondering what was going on with me. Actually, my body was reacting and grieving from the death of my father while my mind was trying to cope with the situation.

After the funeral and resting at home, I fell into a deep depression by not talking to anyone, often putting on a pretend smile trying to hide what was really going on inside my sadden heart: hurt, pain, defeat and loneliness. People deal with depression in various ways. Some just tune out everything and everybody as a way to cope. Some people refer to a professional such as a psychologist to offer solutions to

> The Lord also will be a refuge for the oppressed, a refuge in times of trouble (Psalms 9:9 kjv).

depression but more than often session after session they usually end up with no relief or long-term remedy and all so often leaving the psychologist office with only a huge bill and an appointment scheduled for the next visit. Psychologist teaches you how to deal with depression and various illnesses but, God teaches us how to defeat it!

We see in the book of Matthews where it says:

> "Come unto me, all ye that labour and are heavy laden, and I will give you rest. Take my yoke upon you and learn of me; for I am meek and lowly in heart: and ye shall find rest unto your souls. For my yoke is easy, and my burden is light" (Matt. 11:28-30 kjv).

King David is described in the Bible as the third king of the United Monarch of Israel and, a mighty man of war. Author of many of the Psalms written, King David often spoke about himself suffering from fear of the enemy, being lonely and the grief he suffered from the loss of his sons. But even while going through his many struggles and battles King David reacts in a positive way. He says that, "Surely goodness and mercy shall follow me all the days of my life and I will dwell in the house of the Lord forever." But, how can we truly say that to ourselves when our children are sick and we can't do anything about it, how can we say "Surely goodness and mercy shall follow me all the days of my life" when we are living on the streets, how can we say that after losing a loving spouse or the one person who was closest to us? Your biggest testimony will come from your most difficult battles you had to endure and overcame! But, where do we find the strength to battle suffering and loneliness to respond like David did? The answer is in GOD and in Him alone!

> "Why are you downcast, O my soul? Why so disturbed within me? Put your hope in God for I will yet praise Him, my Savior and my God" (Psalms 42:11 kjv).

The Bibles says, "For your fellowship in the gospel from the first day until now; Being confident of this very thing, that He which hath begun a good works in you will perform it until the day of Jesus Christ:" Meaning that God created you in his own image which is considered good works and if He started it, He is faithful to complete that good works which is you. We have to get out of the mindset of depression, out of the mindset that we are not good enough, out of the mindset that we will never amount to anything because we are made in the image of the King of Kings, the Lord of Lords, The God almighty! Sometimes you may need to widen your vision. Your vision will be greatly impacted by whom you associate with or your surroundings.

Just how limited is your vision? Some time ago, a small boy looked at a well of water for years with visions and thinking of all the possibilities of what he could do with the well of water. Then one day he climbed a tower and he saw a pond. He climbed a little higher and saw a river and then he climbed higher and saw the ocean. He then realized his visions and possibilities of water were

> Now unto him that is able to do exceedingly abundantly above all that we ask or think, according to the power that worketh in us. (Eph. 3:20 kjv)

so unlimited. Over time, he eventually used the surrounding waters to build a windmill which created energy for his household.

God has a blessing for you and you may not even know where it is going to come from. Let's take a quick look at the book of Ruth. It was Ruth's daily routine to go to the nearby field and gather leftover corn to feed the family. We find that after the reapers had gathered all the ears of corn from the fields, Ruth would from sunup till sundown come along after the reapers and gather what was left over on the ground. Still Ruth had little to fill her bag.

Boaz saw her one day and told her to not gather from other fields to continue to gather from this particular field which was his. But what Ruth did not know was that Boaz ahead of time had told the reapers that when they gather the ears of corn to purposely leave a little more behind that she may gather. When it was time for Ruth to gather leftover grain, She gathered more than she ever had before and never knew where the blessing came from (Ruth 2:1-17 kjv). God wants to and will bless you and sometimes you may never know where the blessings came from, it came from God! God has already made provisions for you to prosper.

So, how can we categorize what depression is? I thought about it and came up with three distinct areas:

1. External pressures getting inside your heart when you are down.
2. Mental and physical symptoms that interfere with an individual's ability to function day-to-day.
3. Stress and pressure coming from internal negative thoughts.

Consider this:

* What are you exposing yourself to that is causing you to feel a certain way?
* What are you watching that is affecting your feelings?
* Do you need to separate yourself from certain people?

Today, right now there are so many people who are dealing with the spirit of depression and probably do not even realize it. What really causes one to feel depressed? When you find yourself being depressed it will be a good idea to first find the source. Where did all this depression come from, why am I suddenly feeling like I do? Maybe it is the loss of a loved one. Maybe it is the feeling that no one cares about you or you are not good enough. Perhaps all your children have left home and you for the first time feel all alone. Then all of a sudden you find yourself talking to yourself.

Talking to yourself is a dangerous thing because whatever the situation is, could be an argument with someone, a debate over an issue, when you talk to yourself it is dangerous because you will always come out on top or as being the one who is absolutely right. Depression is a feeling that will try to control you and you will always find yourself in the pits. Whatever the case may be, depression is real when all you want is a breakthrough. Believe me when I say to you that the good Lord will always provide a solution to anything you go through in life. You will get through this! Just hang in there a little while longer.

We walk around feeling sorry for ourselves, feeling lower than lower, miserable and afraid, why? Are you so terrified of what satin will do to harm you? Listen here, you are being afraid of someone who does not even have the keys to his own house! Don't you ever forget that God is the way to overcoming! And He alone holds the keys of life and death (Rev. 1:18 kjv).

> "There hath no temptation taken you but such as is common to man: but God is faithful, who will not suffer you to be tempted above that ye are able, but will with the temptation also make a way to escape, that ye may be able to bear it"
>
> (1Cor. 10:13 kjv).

God is so good, that He will never put more on you than you can bare. Even when you are going through your worst times of your life and you feel that there is no way out, God will be there to give you peace to bear it and provide you a way out, Halleluiah!

Many regard depressions as an illness while others consider depression as evidence of a person having spiritual weakness. Once you are able to recognize the source of depression and as to why you are feeling the way you do then maybe you will be more able to deal with it more clearly and be more equipped to overcome it more quickly.

We read in the Bible where it talks about depression and it refers to depression in such ways as, "one being down casted, having anxiety, weary or even heavy burdened." One of the symptoms of this disease is the feeling of "hopelessness." I am telling you that Hopelessness is a hard one to deal with. Something tragic,

> Thou hast turned for me my mourning into dancing: thou hast put of my sackcloth and girded me with gladness. (Psalms 30:11 kjv).

something that suddenly occurs that leaves you feeling like "This cannot be happening to me and I just want to give up." A sense of feeling that you are alone, all your options are gone, and you have no one to turn to or even talk to. But even while going through perhaps some of the toughest times in your life, you must try to deal with the symptom's in a positive way. God has the best life ahead of you so start living it. You must find your peace and joy where it exists. It may come in the form of either reading a good book, traveling, or simply spending time with friends. Where do you find most joy and peace in your life? You may have to start surrounding yourself around people who are dreamers, around those who have big expectations and big hopes and avoiding small-minded people. Only small-minded people get jealous and try to keep you down.

Think about it, has there ever been a situation He could not fix or a time when God was not there? Even through the most difficult times of your life, God was there to see you through.

Ask yourself a few questions:

1. What three things do I want to accomplish in life?
2. Am I in the job that I want to be doing in ten years from now?
3. What do I feel passionate about?
4. What do others think that I am good at?
5. Who is the one person who I know the best who can give me wise counsel?

Think about where you have been and visualize where you want to go in life. It is important to keep your hope and faith in the Lord.

This is a good time to surround yourself with like-minded people, surround yourself with prayer warriors and build yourself a prayer team. A prayer team does not always have to consist of twenty to thirty people. All you need is a few faithful people whom you can call upon day or night for prayers, ones who will pray and agree with you in prayers especially when you are going through tough struggles.

Facing trials with a positive attitude is simply faith. Keep your head up and remember that God will provide peace and comfort no matter what the issue. He even says in the book of Isaiah to "fear not that He will strengthen and help us and uphold us with His right hand" (Isaiah 41:10 kjv).

Jesus is our healer and a sure comforter. Sometimes we may even have to speak out loud to our storm the same way Jesus did when He spoke to the storm and immediately the storm ceased:

> "And the same day, when the even was come, Jesus saith unto them, Let us pass over to the other side. And when they had sent away the multitude, they took him even as he was in the ship. And there were also with him other little ships.
>
> And there arose a great storm of winds, and the waves beat into the ship, so that it was now full. And he was in the hinder part of the ship, asleep on

a pillow: and they awake him, and say unto him, Master, carest thou not that we perish?

And Jesus arose, and rebuked the wind, and said unto the sea, Peace, be still. And the wind ceased, and there was a great calm. And he said unto them, why are ye so fearful? How is it that ye have no faith?

And they feared exceedingly, and said one to another, What manner of man is this, that even the wind and the sea obey him?" (Mark 4:39 kjv)

Every believer has a voice and that is the voice of victory! Do not just talk about the problems but speak to the problems. Speak to sickness, speak to pain, speak to troubles in your life. God has given you complete authority and a voice to tell that spirit of loneliness, that spirit of hopelessness, that spirit of depression you have to GO! and the devil will have no defense against you.

PRAYER:

"Spirit of defeat, you have no place in me, you have no control or authority over my mind, body or my soul. Evil spirit of torment you have no choice but to GO! I Speak life over my mind, I speak life over my body. I am a child of the Highest King of Kings and I declare restoration and a complete healing over and in me, in Jesus name I pray, amen."

Reflection and Chapter Questions

1. At what times during your life are you most depressed?
2. In this chapter we talked about Boaz and Ruth. In what ways can you apply Boaz's attitude towards Ruth in your own life?

3. Is there a certain person in your life whom you can turn to when you are down and out?

4. When you are depressed how does it affect others who are also depressed?

5. How do you pray yourself out of and overcome a depressed spirit?

RSEARCH QUESTION:

Why did King David arrange the death of Uriah the Hittite? Note: You can find the answer at the end of the book

CHAPTER 9

RACIAL INJUSTICE

There is neither Jew nor Greek, there is
Neither bond nor free, there is neither
Male nor female: for ye are all one in
Christ Jesus.

--(Galatians 3:28 kjv)

The Great Civil Rights leader and Baptist Minister Dr. Martin Luther King Jr. was known for fighting for civil rights. From the mid 1950's until his assassination in 1968, Dr. King sough for equality and human rights especially for African Americans. He was known for delivering his message through many powerful speeches. One speech in particular (I have a dream) he emphasized that he has a dream that one day all men will live in a nation where people would rise up and all would be considered equal. He also mentioned during that speech that he has a dream that one day all of God's children regardless of race, religion or creed would one day join hands.

His main point was that if a nation was ever going to be considered a great nation it had to become true to itself.

Today we celebrate Dr. Martin Luther King for his eloquent speeches, miles and miles of walking for justice and peace but, what about his own personal standards? He had very high standards when it came to spreading God's Word. He had very high standards when it came to education. Dr. Martin Luther King had very high standards when it came to racial equality for all races not just for his. He was a man of dreams and standards. He taught us that when we stand together in peace and in unity that one day we would overcome!

Martin Luther King Died in the year 1968 and believe it or not living here in the year 2020 almost sixty years later, as a nation and as a people we are still wondering if that dream has ever come true or come to pass.

You might say "Yes, we have overcome" because in the year of 1968 the nation awarded its first ever African American Tennis player to win the US Open. You might say "Yes we have overcome" because in the year 2004 we elected the first African American to be President of the United States. That is all good but, at the same time people are still marching in the streets protesting for equal civil rights!

In this very year 2020, African Americans are fighting for the removal of Confederate statues that are still standing and confederate flags that are still waving! Have we really overcome?

You have to admit it that we as a nation have become more divided than ever in the areas of Politics, economics, racial and more importantly when it comes to our spiritually.

> "Now I beseech you, brethren, mark them which cause divisions and offences contrary to the doctrine which ye have learned; and avoid them. For they that are such serve not our Lord Jesus Christ, but their own belly; and by good words and fair speeches deceive the hearts of the simple"(Romans 16:17-18 kjv).

So, why are so many people divided as such and why do some people even the ones whom you attend church with each Sunday, the ones whom you work with and depend on them to do their job choose to live that way? We are all God's people! The sad thing about it is that we are living in a nation where it only takes one incident between two different races for the entire country to become divided.

There was a time many years ago, I think that I was barely out of my teen years when one of my Dad's friend was visiting our home and the topic of racism came up between the two of them and how it was affecting our neighborhoods at that time. He turned to me and said something that has stuck with me over the years. He said, "Paul Jr. there is one thing that I can appreciate about the Ku Klux Clan." I looked at him wondering what he could possibly be talking about.

My Dad's friend continued and said, "I can show a little appreciation to the Ku Klux Clan because at least with them I know where I stand. I know how they feel, and I know their total dislike for certain races. The worse type of people in the world are the ones who will smile in your face, shake your hand and even at times may even give you a hug but, in their hearts they have a problem with you moving into their neighborhoods, moving up in the world and not to mention marrying their children." Whatever kind of way you want to look at it, that is pure racism!!

Racism is evil but there is a difference between things considered as being evil and things being considered as deep evil! You call things evil when they are against God's word. Deep evil is when a person consider evil things as being good. I often wonder what this world would look like if we all loved each other.

Racism is actually the opposite revelation of God! Racism did not start in our generation, but it can end with us right now!

It was not until I was a little older that I actually came to realize and understand as to why when we went on vacations or trips that my Mom would always prepare food beforehand (fried chicken in a shoe box was my favorite) and that we never stopped to eat at restaurants. As an adult I once asked my Dad "Why we never stopped to eat inside a restaurant while traveling?" Simple fact was as my Dad explained, "We couldn't." If not for us gassing up our car or occasional rest area stops, we probably would have driven straight through from Ohio to Georgia.

Why do we treat people so mean and so disrespectful? Seems like even today people judge you based on your race, how you are dressed or even the emblem displayed on the front of your car's hood. No matter how the car looks, it is the emblem that says it all. Take the cheapest car on the car lot and place a Mercedes-Benz emblem in the front of it and people will think differently of the person driving it.

You can walk into an establishment and you are already perceived to be or going to act in a certain way just by the way you look or how you are dressed. Discrimination in any form is just wrong!

Read: James chapter 2:1-13 kjv

Have you ever thought that just maybe you are not giving a particular person a fair chance? I once walked into a jewelry store searching for a gift for my wife. Immediately, I was given crazy looks and uncomfortable stares and I basically felt like the people behind the counter wanted me to leave. I walked around the jewelry store for about five minutes being totally ignored.

But, the very instant it was found out that I had a ten-thousand-dollar credit limit in the store their whole attitude and perception towards me changed. I was instantly being treated like royalty and you would have thought that they were going to put a robe around my shoulders and a crown upon my head. People of all races do not want any special attention or treatment; they just want to be treated equally and fairly that is all. Is that asking too much?

So, How do we overcome racial discrimination? How do we really start to love each other the way God loves us? How do we as a nation begin to start treating each other the way we want to be treated and we can eventually begin to start building a bridge of understanding each other? We first have to have a willingness to change! People will try to put stipulations or requirements on you in order for you to be accepted but, that is not what God wants! Racism has existed since the beginning of time, question is, how do we overcome it? What do you do when you don't know what to do? You call upon the name of the Lord! In Christ alone lies the answer.

Jesus never put requirements or stipulations on who can come to Him!

Jesus simply says, "Come to me" (Matt. 11:28 kjv)

* Bring Racial division to me!
* Bring Economic failures to me!
* Bring your Addictions to me!

Truthfully, it starts with you! You alone can make a difference and you alone can make a change but it starts with Christ. If you personally come to Jesus, He will meet you at whatever stage of life you may be going through right now. You may have a drug addiction, Just come as you are! You may be homeless, Just come as you are! You may have lost a loved one and has given up on life spiritually and mentally, Just come as you are! You may have a problem with discriminating people, Just come as you are because Jesus is the solution for every issue you or the world may be dealing with.

It has been several years ago, before my wife and I left Ohio that there was an incident between a Caucasian police officer and a young African American man. Whatever occurred between the two ended up leaving the police officer on a two-week paid leave during the investigation and the young black man dead.

Without even hearing all the facts and details of what actually took place between the two or even considering who was right or wrong, within hours the entire community had become divided over the matter. Lord have mercy on us! Majority of the Caucasian citizens had supported the police officer and the African American community was supporting the young black man.

It is no doubt that for decades people of the minority or people of color have faced many areas of structural barriers such as obtaining quality housing, healthcare, employment and let us not forget education.

You remember the story of Jesus when He was heading to Galilee had stopped through the town of Samaritan where Jacob's well was located. Being tired from His long travel, Jesus sat by Jacob's well. A Samaritan woman came to draw water: Jesus saith unto her, "Give me to drink (John 4:7 kjv)." When she looked at the clothes Jesus was wearing and noticed the color of His skin, she knew that Jesus was a Jew and was shocked when Jesus asked for a drink of water.

Even though the Samaritans were half-Jews and half-Gentiles the Jews did not associate with the Samaritans. She already had a preconceived opinion of who Jesus was by His clothing and skin color and she felt that they were not to associate with each other. But, pointing to the well of water during the conversation Jesus said "Whosoever drinketh of this water shall thirst again: But whosoever drinketh of the water that I shall give him shall never thirst; but the water that I shall give him shall be in him a well of water springing up into everlasting life" (John 4:11-14 kjv).

The woman saith unto Jesus, "Sir, give me this water, that I thirst not, neither come hither to draw" (John 4:15 kjv). While the Samaritan woman at the well initially had her mind on the physical water and looking at skin color and clothes, Jesus was trying to introduce the Samaritan woman to a spiritual reality and eventually she began to understand.

In the same chapter, we see that the same thing happened with Jesus disciples. After coming from the city to buy meat to eat they cometh to Jesus saying, "Master, eat" (John 4:31).

But Jesus said unto them, "I have meat to eat that ye know not of" (John 4:32 kjv). The disciples deliberated among themselves, "Hath any man brought Jesus to eat" (John 4:32 kjv). The disciples had thought that someone else had brought Jesus something to eat. The point is that just like the Samaritan woman at the well, the disciples were looking at things from a physical point of view while Jesus was speaking from a spiritual perspective!

We too so often get confused not knowing whether to look at thinks from a spiritual aspect or from a physical perspective. Just like the Corona Virus the entire world is trying to figure out things from a physical point of view with the mask, people separation from each other, sanitizer and everything else but the one thing we are over looking at is that maybe we need to start fighting this virus from a spiritual point of view with a spiritual God!

We were made in the image of the almighty God! We are all children of a common God! Our blood is the same color, our money is the same color but somewhere throughout time we have obtained the mindset that based on the outward appearance of a particular individual they are already prejudged accordingly. If I am not mistaken somewhere in my Bible, it states that we are not to judge one another.

> "Let us not therefore judge one another anymore: but judge this rather, that no man put a stumbling-block or an occasion to fall in his brother's way" (Romans 14:13 kjv).

Whether you want to realize it or not, we must learn to live together on this earth. One week, people are peacefully marching for human rights and the next week there are hate signs popping up everywhere, riots and more than ever nationwide public killings! We need to stop making excuses. Our American values

> There is neither Jew nor Greek, there is neither slave nor free, there is no male and female, for you are all one in Christ Jesus. Galatians 3:28 kjv

and constitutional rights are for all of us. The solution is clear…Stop the generational taught hate, systematic racism, and unequal application of laws. Stop killing people especially young black men. How many times must the past be repeated to learn the lesson… Maybe that hateful spirit of discrimination was passed down to you.

Your parents were that way, their parents were that way but, I'm here to tell you: That spirit of discrimination, that spirit of racism, that spirit of hate can stop with you! You can make a difference! You have to teach your children that yes there are different races and people do look differently but, we are all the same and we should all be treated the same.

You don't have to read no further than the book of Genesis to realize that racism existed even during biblical times but history has proven to us that our world is a better place to live in when men and women of good character stand together against hate, fear, injustice and the evil acts of those who seek to divide us. Mutual respect for one another is key as we are equally responsible for the legacy our generation leaves for the next.

The Bible also says that:

> "I do not speak to condemn you, for I have said before that you are in our hearts to die together and to live together" (2 Cor. 7:3 kjv).

What do you not understand about that? I am referring to myself as well because I have a lot of issues that I am still working out. We are not born with racism and a judgmental heart. Example, you can put five children of five different races in a play pen and they will get alone and play together just fine all day. It is not until they get a little older that they begin to notice the different perspectives of how people treat each other. On how people respect or disrespect another person based on the color of their skin. Slowly that mindset of racism begins developing into their pure and innocent heart and mind.

The terrible thing about this dreadful mindset is that the children begin to actually believe that this form of behavior is normal and acceptable! I tell you that these actions and destructive behaviors of people if not dealt with properly is passed down to the next generation and the spirit of racism continues. We have many different races and cultures in this world and believe it or not, it only takes the efforts of one race to stand up to put their foot down and say "This will stop NOW" to defeat the spirit of racism that exist today.

> *"No one is born hating another person because of the colour of his skin or his background, or his religion. People must learn to hate, and if they can learn to hate, they can be taught to love, for love comes more naturally to the human heart than its opposite."* -Nelson Mandela

Race does not define a person's level of intelligence nor does it define who you are. You better be careful how you treat people because you just might be mistreating or entertaining an angel unaware!

We are on this earth together, and God has put us here for a reason mostly to "be fruitful and multiply, fill the earth and subdue it; have dominion (Gen. 1:28 kjv). But there are so many things that we have absolutely no control over in the matter. You had absolutely no control on the day in which you were born or your race. You had no control in the matter of who your parents were going to be! You can even look at this from a bigger point of view. You have no control of when the sun comes up or when it goes down. You have no control over the tides of the seas when it ebbs and flows each day. But one thing that you do have control over and that is how you treat your fellow man.

Why are we so divided? We were not designed or created to fight each other, argue about senseless things like what religion or where you live or what type of job you hold. When my wife and I first moved to Texas, we were asked where we lived? Our response was, "Tyler." The next question was, "What part of Tyler?" Unknowingly, at that very moment we were being prejudged and put in a particular category. No one knew where we had come from, our level of income or our level of educational experience.

Reason is those things only matter to us and not to the Father. In heaven those things are useless! We spend way entirely too much of our precious time trying to figure out things that has absolutely no value to you or the Father!

Believe me when I say that:

> "When you begin to understand the nature of a person you will never be surprised by their behavior or their action!"

Maybe you need to get to know a person personally first before placing judgement upon them. How are you going to dislike a person based on what someone else said about them or what you heard through the grapevine about them? The only antidote and answer to racism is Jesus Christ! Our focus is to live a Christ Like life and to live peaceably with others. Our lives should reflect the love

> A new command I give you: Love one another. As I have loved you, so you must love one another. By this everyone will know that you are my disciples, if you love one another.
> John 13:34-35 kjv

and righteousness of Christ that is shown within us. Would you agree? Eliminating racial prejudice is in us and in our society is not going to be easy but demands introspection and effort.

Why is it so hard to simply love each other? We need to reject any racial tendencies as well as engage and educate those who propagate racial insensitivity and bigotry and with the help of the good Lord, this behavior will be defeated!!! Racism is the opposite revelation of God!

Racism did not start in our generation, but it can end with us right now! I don't know God's plan regarding how He is going to deal with this, but one thing that I do know is this: If we follow God's Word, He will lead all of us to that place in life who God referred to in the book of Exodus-The promise land-that place considered as the goal towards which Christians journey in their earthly lives. A place of happiness or fulfilment, racial reconciliation, and racial unity. When we are silent regarding racism, we are actually speaking very loudly! What we all need is simply this: MORE LOVE!

In this chapter we tried to focus on racial injustice but, I have to keep in mind that we all are dealing with other personal issues as well on a daily basis which seem almost impossible to overcome. If we all come to Jesus and lay down our burdens whether it be racial discrimination, bigotry or whatever and lay those burdens down at the foot of the cross, Jesus will fix it! That is a promise of God! We all need to be more like Christ! Every person should be treated the same regardless of how you feel or what you think about them because you can never know when you just might be entertaining angels!

Reflection and Chapter Questions

1. In what ways has your race affected your life?
2. Why do you feel that there are so many people divided when it comes to race?
3. What incident in your life was racially motivated?
4. In this chapter Paul talks about the Samaritan Woman at the well how she prejudged Jesus by the color of His skin and the clothes He was wearing, has there been a time in your life where you were in the same position as the Samaritan woman and wrongly prejudged someone?
5. How can we as a nation overcome racial discrimination or where do we start?

RSEARCH QUESTION:

We find that The Promise Land is mentioned in this chapter. Question: Who are the only ones to who actually made it into The Promise Land? Hint, there were only two.

Note: You can find the answer at the end of the book

CHAPTER 10

WORLDWIDE EPIDEMIC

"Watch out that no one deceives you. For many will come in my name, claiming, "I am the Messiah; and will deceive many. You will hear of wars and rumors of wars but see to it that you are not alarmed. Such things must happen, but the end is still to come. Nation will rise against nation, and kingdom against kingdom. There will be famines and earthquakes in various places."

----(MATTHEW 24-4-7 kjv

All throughout the Holy Bible you will find that God gives prophesies to His people. Prophecies of inspiration, of interpretation and predictions but of the thousands of beautiful scriptures and prophesies written in the Holy Bible, there is one prophesy that stands out more than all the rest letting us know that in the

> For the weapons of our warfare are not carnal, but mighty through God to the pulling down of strong holds.
> 1 Corinthians 10 :4 kjv

present day we are in a war. Now please understand my dear reader that God did not give prophesies to scare His people but to warn us so that we could be prepared for what was to come. God prophesized over two thousand years ago that we will hear of wars and rumors of wars and I am here to tell you that the world in which we are living in today, we as a nation are dealing with a war! Not just any kind of war, this war is different. We are dealing with a war not fought with guns or heavy artillery or anything like that, but a war that needs to be fought spiritually.

When a virus exists and attacks the physical body, you can't see it even with a microscope, it is in the air, on everything you touch causing everyone to wear facial mask and top scientist are baffled and have no clue on a solution. This is an invisible enemy! Believe me when I tell you that an invisible enemy is much more dangerous than an enemy you can see! When you can actually see your enemy, you could have an edge and an advantage over them and possibly a fighting chance. But when the enemy is invisible, you have no one to fight, they have the advantage over you and pretty much you have lost the battle before it starts. My dear reader from watching the news and hearing about things going on in the world we need to have spiritual discernment to be able to distinguish what is spiritual and what is physical.

> For we wrestle not against flesh and blood,
> But against principalities, against powers,
> Against the rulers of the darkness of this
> World, against spiritual wickedness in high
> Places. ---Ephesians 6:12 kjv

Storms can be described in either of three different forms:

* Spiritual
* Physical
* Mental

You might ask "Paul, why do you say that?" Well, at the present time we as a nation are experiencing at storm unlike any the world has ever experienced in history. This particular storm has come in the form of a virus so called The Coronavirus. When this virus first appeared on the scene a lot of people were not really concerned about it especially since it was confined to a country over seven thousand miles away from the US. Many felt that this particular country would come up with a cure and handle the situation and it would not even come close to United States and the virus would be a thing of the past.

But such was not the case, Lord have mercy on us, it did reach the United States and with this corona virus even the most dedicated desired scientist and biologist in the world had no clue as to how to handle it or what to do to solve it.

When God created man, He gave man dominion over all the earth. God has given us authority, power and dominion over all the earth but, how can we utilize that power to solve an issue when we really don't have a clear understanding of it?

The Bible says that:

> "Wisdom is the principal thing; therefore, get wisdom: and with all thy getting get understanding."
> Proverbs 4:7 kjv

We as a nation do not have a clue regarding this Corona Virus as to how it developed, how to stop it, and more importantly having an antidote that will fight against it to keep hundreds of people from dying from it!

This virus was different because it not only was unfamiliar to everyone, but it also had the capability to change its configuration and multiply itself meaning that as soon as scientist felt that a cure was on the horizon, the virus would change its configuration making it even harder to come up with a cure. This was one battle that could not be overcome or won with guns, tanks, bombs, or any type of ammunition stored up.

People panicked as many began to die. Over time the world had over 1.2 million people die from this virus with no sure treatment in sight. Leaders in high positions, The President of the US, Prime Ministers, and Scientist from all around the world put their heads together and felt that the only way to slow down the virus from spreading further was to separate people's contact from each other by putting yourself at least six feet away from each other, no touching, washing hands constantly and to top it all off there was a country wide alert that stated you had to stay in your house until further notice unless it was a dire necessity like getting food or medicines. This is all against what the word of God says. The Bible also says "That if two of you shall agree on earth as touching anything that they shall ask; it shall be done for them of my Father which is in heaven (Matthew 18:19). How can we touch and agree on anything if we are required to stand six feet apart from each other?

To top things off and to make things even worst, all churches were to close. What do you mean all churches closed? Yes, even the churches closed no matter the denomination Baptist, Catholic, Pentecostal it did not matter yes, all churches closed! I never understood that! I never understood that how you could close all churches but kept places open like Planned Parenthood open. You closed all churches but not only kept the place open but gave them federal monies to keep them open! You want to close the very place where people are crying out on their knees for the Lord to step in and heal our nation, but you fight to keep open the very place where they are killing babies at an enormous rate each day, but you want to close the churches! This too is against what the word of God says. The Bible says that we should "Not forsake the assembly of ourselves together" (Hebrew 10:25 kjv)." Because this virus was everywhere (in the air) and on everything (you touch) many felt that this virus was not only something the entire world was unfamiliar with but it was also considered to be spiritual! So, what do you do when you don't know what to do? You call upon the name of the Lord!

Think about this: What if we as a country instead of practicing social distancing we practiced touching and agreeing that this virus would be defeated and we start praying together. What if we all took off the mask and cried out and proclaimed "We need help Lord; this is beyond us!" Just maybe this virus would become a thing of the past and we all would know for a fact and have no doubt that Jesus is Lord! But still here we are trying to figure out a solution on our own without the help of the Lord.

At the present time what we are failing to realize is that we are fighting a spiritual battle, so we need one who is Spiritual to defeat it. The fact of the matter is that this is a time when the entire world needs God to step in and eradicate this virus because man has no solution. Never in my fifty-seven years of living on this earth have I ever experienced such a time as this. This Worldwide epidemic is a wakeup call. Hundreds of people dying each day is a reminder and a promise to all that tomorrow is not promised to anyone.

Talk about bringing one down to their knees to where you have nothing or no one to depend on but GOD, yes this is that period in time. People are required to stay home. People are required to stay six feet apart from each other. People are required to cover their faces with a mask. Through all of this God is still working! You tell me something, what better way can God make time for you to pray and worship more? What better way can God provide for you time to increase your communing with Jesus! What better time than now do we have to get to know Jesus Christ on a higher spiritual level? God is still working and turning a negative situation into a positive one!

I found that spending more time alone with God allowed Him to speak to me more clearly through His Word. This had become a time of rejoicing! A time to reflect on my life where I could receive answers and revelations from heaven! Right now, Jesus is teaching me how to draw closer to him and that is what we all need right now and that is to hear His voice and learn how to draw closer to the Father.

This pandemic also required my wife and I to remain in our house alone together day in and day out twenty-four hours a day for three weeks. Usually we would go off on our separate ways either to work or wherever and not see each other for several hours or so. Even on weekends we would spend quality time together, but this was different. Married men you know what I mean. My wife and I have been married for over thirty-four years and empty nesters for over fifteen years, but this seemed different.

The first couple of days together in our home was normal but after a week or so, I began to watch her as she would come around the corner dancing, praising, and singing worship songs with huge smiles on her face like never before. Me, I sat in my recliner watching TBN and the various sermons that came on. I like to hear Pastors Tony Evans, TD Jakes and Joel Osteen. I was going on as usual, but my wife was really taking positive advantage over the present situation we were experiencing.

Outside our home doors is complete pandemonium, stores closed for weeks, many without food, I actually saw two ladies fighting over a roll of tissue in the store, people scrambling just to survive! But my wife was rejoicing, singing, worshipping, and really crying out to the Lord when praying!

> "Rejoice in the Lord always; again, I say Rejoice." ---PHILIPPIANS 4:4kjv

Yes, we did our morning prayers together, yes, we called various ones and prayed for them, yes, we spent most of the day given to the Lord. But it seemed to me that she went beyond what we usually did.

I once asked my wife Elaina what her definition of a storm was. Her answer was right to the point and simple. "A storm is something that happens to you or around you that you are not prepared for and you need God to intervene."

When I thought about what she had said it made me think. It brought to mind one of the worst storms my family ever had to endure. It happened years ago when our eldest child was only five years old was walking holding my hand. Our middle daughter was on my shoulder and our youngest daughter was in a stroller. The snow had accumulated up to four feet and we all had to walk an entire block in the snow to get to our home because our van had gotten stuck in the snow.

But my wife was thinking deeper than a weather storm,
she was speaking from a spiritual point of view.
"A storm is something that happens to you or around you that
you are not prepared for and you need God to intervene."

Truly, my dear reader, this is the time when we should be doing more and going out and beyond what is the usual or what we normally do.

Right now, we are experiencing a world around us unlike anything we have ever had to endure. What do you do when you don't know what to do? You call upon the name of the Lord!

Let me ask you a simple question:

"Would you agree that the Word of God is missed somewhere?" In the school systems, in your work place and yes even in the church. The presence of GOD seems to be not as important as before. Has all this taking GOD out of everything finally come to a point. There used to be a time when prayer was allowed in schools, but that was taken out. GOD has been taken out of public events; you get funny looks from people even when you pray before eating! What the heck! The WORD of GOD still stands.

Think about this, many people build up their bodies with various vitamins which is always good. Many are trying to start eating right and so on but, what about building up the most important aspect of your life, building up your soul. If we can allow our spirit to align up with our soul, Jesus will begin to do a work in our lives. You will begin to see miracles after miracles happening all around you at times when you least expect them.

There were major epidemics that occurred even during biblical times. We see even in the book of Genesis where the Bible shows that when we ignore HIS presence and disregard HIS will, He will show us that HE is the only true and living GOD.

During the days of Moses after the old Pharaoh had died a new Pharaoh appeared on the throne, the Israelites were still being held as slaves. While being in the land of Midian, Moses goes to Mount Horeb where Yahweh appeared to him in a burning bush. GOD'S WORD to Moses was to go to Egypt to free the Hebrew slaves and to lead them to the promise land. Moses did what he was instructed to do but, this new Pharaoh's heart was hardened and refused to let the children of Israel go free.

After the many plagues and disaster's that occurred in Egypt like the river turning into blood, infestation of frogs and locust Pharaoh eventually decided to let the Israelites go free but, if you remember reading the story of Moses, Pharaoh's heart was hardened, so instead of freeing the Israelites, he decided to pursue after them to kill them! On one side the Israelites were faced with the mighty Red Sea and on the other side was Pharaoh's army the Egyptians hastily chasing after them. What were the Israelites to do? What do you do when you don't know what to do? You call upon the name of the Lord! Just like that God stepped in and opened up the Red Sea and made a highway of dry land through the Red Sea so that the Israelites could safely pass through the waters to get to the other side.

GOD gave Pharaoh many opportunities to follow His WORD, but Pharaoh constantly refused. GOD had to prove to him and show him through many tragic events that HE meant what HE said. In the end Pharaoh lost his son, his entire army and eventually fell to his knees and cried out "HIS GOD (referring to Moses God) IS GOD!"

Moses relied on GOD, heard HIS voice, and obeyed. I ask you; how often do you hear the Lord's voice? How often do you listen and obey HIS instructions and follow them? Sometimes GOD will have to make things quite simple and plain and clear to us for us to come to our senses. You may not know what HE is saying, or you may not know what HE is doing in your life but, believe me when I tell you that HE knows what is best for you and will not lead you down the wrong path.

Earlier in this chapter we talked about the corona virus that is at the present time affecting the entire world. It brought to mind a friend of mine who recently had a conversation with a prominent doctor. He asked the doctor "What is going on with this corona virus?" And the sad thing about it was that after talking with the doctor for a while he realized that he had as much information and knowledge about the corona virus as the doctor did. The plain truth is that nobody really knows what is going on.

So, what do you do when you don't know what to do? You call upon the name of the Lord! We are told to wear a mask over our face and practice social distance but is that the answer? No, we need God!

Prayer is the key and, in these days, praying can sometimes be the only option left. Family is gone. Layed off from job. On the verge of being homeless. Only recourse left, and the most important of all is Praying. Prayer will activate the will of God in your life. When we come together as saints and really cry out to the Lord for help and for our needs, I promise that HE will answer and come through. God is speaking to you today. He knew that you would need a healing, encouragement, or a simple word from Him that would give direction, comfort, or inspiration that everything was going to be all right.

He wants you to know that He is able and that He is right there by your side! You don't need to be afraid of the many tragic issues that are occurring in the world just trust God, He is able to see you through anything and carry you through any negative situation you may face. Do not worry!

> Fear thou not; for I am with thee: be not dismayed; for I am thy God: I will strengthen thee; yea, I will uphold thee with the right hand of my righteousness (Isaiah 41:10 kjv).

At that very moment when you think all hope is gone and you feel you have no other options, just like when He told the Israelites to "GO FORWARD" (Ex: 15:14 kjv).

He is speaking to you right now to GO FORWARD!

No matter what you are going through, whatever trial you are facing, "GO FORWARD!"

Because the Lord will give you a path of dry land to make sure you will overcome. "GO FORWARD" because nothing is too hard for God!

Prayer:

Dear Lord, our entire world is suffering like never before. We need Your help in finding a cure for something that we don't understand. We have tried on our own and have failed, please step in and heal your land, in Jesus name I pray, amen.

Reflection and Chapter Questions

1. How do you feel about current events happening in the world today?
2. How do you fight against spiritual things you cannot see?
3. What are some of the storms in your personal life?
4. How did you benefit from the storms?
5. How is God speaking to you during this worldwide epidemic?

RSEARCH QUESTION:

What was the name of the person who first initiated the Hebrew's passage through the Red Sea, by walking in the sea Head-deep until the sea parted?

Note: You can find the answer at the end of the book

CHAPTER 11

OVERCOMING FEAR

For God hath not given us the spirit of fear; but
of power, and love, and of a sound mind."
—(2 Timothy 1:7 kjv)

If you ever think that there will be a time in your life when you will not experience fear, I'm sorry to tell you that you are sadly mistaken. Fear is something that while you are living on this earth and breathing oxygen you will experience some form of fear. It may come in the form of The fear of losing a job, the fear of your health failing, whatever the case may be, during some time throughout your life, you will experience fear.

Fear is a behavior that is taught rather than most belief that it is a natural instinct. You can take a child who has not been taught to fear dogs will walk up to a dangerous pit bull and rub his nose because they have no fear of the dog. You can take a child who has not been taught to fear water will step into a swimming pool not knowing how to swim because they have no fear of water. A child must be taught the dangers of animals, water, height, fire, and such things to prevent them from suffering repercussions and possibly getting hurt.

Sometimes we can become so fearful that the spirit of fear is passed down even to our children. You find a grown man who happened to have had a bad experience in a swimming pool at a young age and had become fearful of not only swimming but of deep water as well. You find a guy who had a bad experience at a young age traveling by plane, now that same guy is an adult and is afraid of heights and will not even climb a ladder. The bad thing about fear is that when you fear something, you always imagine the worst possible thing that can happen in a situation. In reality after it actually happens you realize that it was not as bad as what you were thinking. After I had my most recent surgery, I fret for over six weeks the thought of having the stent taken out. I could not sleep, constantly talking to people who had one taken out, looking at frightening videos of the procedure,

> See that I command thee to be strong and of good courage; be not afraid, neither be thou dismayed; for, the Lord thy God with thee wherever thou goest. (Joshua 1:9 kjv)

it was bad. When the time eventually came to have the stent taken out, it took less than two minutes and I vaguely remember what happened. The terrible thing about these fears or negative behaviors is that when they are exposed around other people especially children, they can sometimes take on that behavior of fear without even experiencing life for themselves. Don't let fear take control over you or stop you from enjoying life.

FEAR OF CHANGE

When my Wife, my three daughters and I first moved into our new neighborhood, one of our main desires and goals was first and foremost was to find a church. Not just any church, we were looking for one that provided a children's ministry, a Wednesday Bible study, a men's, and women's group and possibly some type of outreach ministry. I know that sounds like asking for a lot from one church but, after visiting many churches and communicating with congregations, we found one!

The church was a Pentecostal, which meant that they praised and worshipped the way we were accustomed to. My children made many friends at the church and I became part of the music ministry which I deeply loved. My wife became a member of the Women's group and the seven of them did their usual activities such as visiting widows, setting up fund raisers and holding events for the church. Everything we could ask or require from a church we were supplied with.

Now, I must let you know that my wife and I love to read and study the Bible every day. Each Monday we open our home to anyone willing to come and spend several hours crying out to the Lord, Praising and worshipping.

Well everything was going well in the church, but something was missing that I could not quite put my finger on. I come to realize that our lovely church did not have or offer weekly Bible study. I did not think that it would be such a big deal to simply ask why the church did not offer Bible study but, it became a big issue. I talked with one of the brothers and asked hm.

He stated that it was a good idea to talk with one of the Assistant Pastors which I did. I even suggested that we could start one lasting only an hour or so. The Assistant Pastor relayed the message. I was ready and eager to finally participate in a weekly Bible study class.

The next Sunday right before the sermon was to be preached another Assistant Pastor took the mike and looking directly at my wife and myself started speaking: "Look here, this church has been in existence for over forty years without ever closing and keeping membership up. Evidently, they must be doing something right! They do not need folks coming in here trying to change things and messing things up! If you feel things are not what you are looking for then maybe this church is not for you." Where is the love? Where is the compassion?

"Love is patient, love is kind, it does not envy, it does not boast, it is not proud, it does not dishonor others, it is not self-seeking, it is not easily angered, it keeps no record of wrongs, Love does not delight in evil but rejoices with truth, it always protects, always trust, always hopes, always perseveres, Love never fails.

1 Corinthians 13:4-8 kjv

I was so startled at what I had just heard that I froze in my seat wondering if my wife was thinking what I was thinking and that was to "get up and walk out." My father taught me at a young age to never give in to intimidation from anyone. Yes, we were offended and a little embarrassed, but we sat there and waited to hear the rest of the sermon.

After the message, a member of my wife's group approached us and asked if we could talk. We followed her to an adjacent room and she immediately started crying right in front of us. She hugged my wife and then said:

"That was completely wrong what he said up there and many of us do not agree with it but, it was not his fault, he was only doing what he was told to do. Let me explain something to the both of you, as you can see when you look around the sanctuary ninety percent of the members are over sixty to seventy years of age. A lot of them are actually original members of this church. We who are much younger members of the church have been

A CHANGE IS COMING!

We will not hide them from their children, shewing to the generation to come the praises of the Lord, and His strength, and His wonderful works that He hath done. For He established a testimony in Jacob, and appointed a law in Israel, which He commanded our fathers, that they should make them known to their children: That the generation to come might know them, even the children which should be born; who should arise and declare them to their children: That they might set their hope in God, and not forget the works of God, but keep His commandments: And might not be as their fathers, a stubborn and rebellious generation; a generation that set not their heart aright, and whose spirit was not steadfast with God(Psalm 78:4-8 kjv).

trying to change the mindset of the older members, but they close their ears to any form of change. We are still singing songs from the seventies and following old traditions. Everything is so routine. When new young people come and are looking for a new church home and after only one service, we do not see them anymore. It has been really hard, but the older members simply refuse change and do not want to hear any new ideas. I am asking you two beautiful people, please don't leave and give us another chance."

My wife and I talked it over and decided to give the church another chance. The following Sunday, we walked in the front door with a few more first-time guests. The same lady that had spoken to us the week before approached us and said, "I am glad that you all have come back. We had a meeting with many of the older members and we had a good meeting."

After praise and worship one of the younger members who looked to be about seventeen or eighteen years old went to the podium and began to speak:

"Every Sunday and it seems like every time the doors of the church opened; my family was here. I graduated from Sunday School, Discipleship and participated in every performance the church ever put on since I was five years old. I dress like you all do; I sing the songs from the song book that is so old that the pages are turning brown. I am now seventeen years old getting ready to go off to college. In one year, I will be an adult making my own decisions. Now, do you really believe that I will be coming back here?"

The church of about eighty members froze in silence.

The young man began to speak again, "My friends listen to current music, we pray totally different than you do, we worship differently than you do. We don't care about what we are wearing, or you have to pray a certain way to be accepted all we care about is God."

"Therefore, if any man be in Christ, he is a new creature:

97

old things are passed away; behold, all things are become new."

---2CORINTHIANS 5:7 kjv

Then unexpectedly one of the older members with his head held down and tears in his eyes politely took the microphone and started to speak.

"You know church, I am one of the original members of this church and I remember when we first broke ground to start building this church over forty some years ago. I believe that we as a church need to start making a lot of changes around here. Several days ago, I took my granddaughter to a Young Christian conference where there was an auditorium full of over two hundred or more teenagers. They praised and worshipped the Lord unlike anything that I have ever seen in my entire life. Whether you want to believe it or not, they are our future. If we do not do something fast and begin to start making some changes at this church, we are going to miss out on an entire generation of future true believers who sincerely love the Lord. They have so much energy and we need that." He went and sat down as his wife gave him a big hug.

The next Sunday I was totally surprised. The older gentlemen member who spoke the previous Sunday had told his Granddaughter to bring all her friends to church and so did many other members had done the same thing. The church for the first time in its history was full to the capacity with standing room only. I was hearing new upbeat songs and the teens could wear what they wanted. As the worship went on, teens were up dancing and praising and worshipping unlike the church had ever seen before. The praise went on for at least an hour past the usual time which did not seem to bother anyone because many of the older members were up dancing, praising, and worshipping as well! Actually, there was no time for the Pastor to give his prepared sermon! We all had a great time in worshipping the Lord!

You cannot ever have a vision even in the church when everything is based on tradition.

"And be ye kind one to another, tenderhearted, forgiving one another, even as God for Christ's sake hath forgiven you" (Ephesians 4:32 kjv).

Even today, the younger generation must forgive the older generation because the older generation has the experience and a lot of wisdom and knowledge. The older generation must find it in their heart to forgive the younger generation because the younger generation has new ideas and a lot of energy.

The problem occurs when the church starts to become just another Sunday routine or everything is based on tradition. Church starts at 10:00am and ends at exactly 12:00pm every Sunday right on time. But, how can you predict when the service will end at a certain time especially when the holy spirit is flowing? If people are praying, worshipping, and are getting healed, why would you want to quench the spirit and stop the service because of a time factor? People are hurting, people are spiritually dying and need a breakthrough which may take hours after church ends.

Now, do not get routine and habit confused. They are not the same. A routine is when you do something based on a specified time, plan, or schedule like I always pray before getting into bed at night. I cut our grass on schedule every third Friday of the month.

A habit is when you do not have any intention on doing something but because you have been doing it for so long the exact same way over time it has become a natural behavior to you. People can have a habit of stealing, lying even speeding while driving never having intentions on doing it. Once you begin to understand the choices you make then you will be able to make changes to the habits you want to get rid of.

A positive habit for me for example is that no matter who the person is, or people are, I always greet them with a smile or handshake especially when I walk into a room full of people and I enter their presence. Some habits can be so hard to overcome

> I can do all things through Christ which strengtheneth me (Phil.4:13 kjv).

that it actually has to take Fast and Praying to overcome it. Fasting is giving up something physical in order to receive something spiritual!

A bad habit that I once had was that I was a nervous fingernail biter for years. I had been biting my fingernails off since the age of six or seven. It had become a natural habit for me. My wife and I fasted and prayed for a week that I would stop the habit of nail biting. I gave up eating snacks for one week and my wife gave up chocolates for one week and we constantly prayed.

This was one habit that I could not control but eventually after much fasting and praying fifty years later I overcame it! Well, I guess that I also have to give a whole lot of credit to my wife because she constantly also reminded me how terrible my fingernails looked and how unattractive it was after I had bitten them.

I guess it is fine to have some routines in your life but, the overall problem arises when our routines become a habit and you have become comfortable. Some of the biggest mistakes we make in lives are:

1. Trying to do things without God's help.
2. Forgetting who we are in Christ Jesus.
3. Have no accountability for our actions.
4. No self-control or cannot stand to be corrected.

God can take you out of your comfort zone and do a new thing in your life if you are willing to open up and receive Him. What God has in store for not only the church but for you as well is in abundance and over exceeds more than what you expect. The bottom line is, we all need more love in our hearts, and we need to hear from the Lord! We serve a God who can do a work in our lives even when we do not realize or have a clue as to what He is doing, or His plan is.

Two of the major issues facing the church today is Pride and selfishness. When you find a church and it does matter the faith whether it be Baptist, Pentecostal, Catholic where members

> Call unto me, and I will answer thee, and show great and mighty things, which thou knowest not.
>
> Jeremiah 33:3 kjv

can actually look down on folks because they are not worshiping the way you do, does not pray the way you do and for sure they don't dress the way you do, yes there is a problem. Not everyone is at the same spiritual level that you are at. When my wife and I first got married in1986, we had a neighbor who was a member of a large church with thousands of members. When we initially visited, we did not notice how everyone was dressed the exact same way. Headscarf's, long dresses, and hair down to their backs. I did not think it was a problem because we became good friends with many of the members. One Sunday our neighbor did not go to church, but we decided to go anyway. I had on a nice suit and my wife had dressed very modestly.

But, almost as soon as we got there, we were approached regarding the way we dressed and prayed, and I suddenly began to feel uncomfortable. Did they realize and understand that we were just visitors and we had only been there a few times? Believe me when I say that I have no problem with dressing modestly and conforming to various church standards, but when you are more or less put in a position where you are not so much as forced but looked down upon for not appearing and looking the way they are, I find that to be an issue. The Bible does not actually say "Come as you are" but the Bible does say:

> *"Come unto me, all ye that labour and are heavy laden, and I will give you rest." Matt. 11:28 kjv*

God does not care about the way you dress or the way you praise and worship, just remember WHO you are praising and WHO you are worshipping! Jesus says to come to me. He cares about your heart and if it is in right standing with Him. He does not care if you are an alcoholic, drug addicted or even if you consider yourself to be the worst of the worst sinners, God will meet you wherever you are in life and receive you with open arms! You are His children. Man looks at the outer appearance, but God looks at the heart.

I truly believe that one should let the love of God capture their heart and speak to them regarding changes and not so much as trying to please a leader of a church or another individual. Yes, I do agree that we must respect our spiritual leaders but do not get it twisted, God is the head of the church. The only one whom we fully honor and give all our praise and worship to is the God of heaven and earth. The God who can heal the sick, who has walked on waters, the God who can raise the dead to life! That is where our alliance and relationship remains, period.

A lot of times it is the mindset and selfish belief of one person leading the entire congregation based on their own personal understanding instead of following Biblical truths. That is when the spirit of pride and selfishness begins to take over. That is when the church starts to follow man's beliefs and not Gods!

Many times, we need to make changes in our personal lives as well. We may need to change our attitude toward loved ones. We may need to change the way we look at situations and get a clearer understanding of it.

Question: What is your life based on or What affects you?

1. Are you a people pleaser? Meaning, do you always say or do things to please people to make them feel happy regardless as to how you end up feeling- sad, miserable unhappy whatever.

2. Are you a Tradition Person? Meaning, do you decide on most things based on the way they have always been done? Thinking, they have been done this way forever and they should work for me now.

3. Do you live based on current feelings? Meaning, do you base things or make decisions based on how you feel at the current moment? Are you an impulsive thinker or an impulsive buyer? If it looks good or feels good, I will do it.

4. Do you rely heavily on the opinion of others? Meaning, do you respect others opinions over your own. When you express

your issues to others, do you expect an answer or response from them that will help you make decisions.

Whatever the case may be, each aspect of life can be detrimental if applied the wrong way.

There may be times a change of our mindset is needed as to the way we look and think about certain issues. Do you sometimes base your choices or opinions on the way a person looks or their race? Having a preconceived opinion that is not based on reason or actual experience is what you would call-prejudice. Have you ever thought that just maybe you were wrong to say what you said or judged someone based on what you heard about them? We all need more love in our heart and one that is open. Try seeing someone with more love because a little love can bring changes.

In all actuality, I honestly believe that a person who is unwilling to discuss possible options or have a closed mind on certain issues is simply harboring a heart and mind full of pride. They do not even want to listen to anybody or what you have to say. They feel and think that their decision is the best one and it is final and yes it happens right there within the church. The only thing you can do in a situation such as that or come across a person like that is to pray for them because it is out of your hand and you alone can do nothing, just pray for them.

> "I will bless the Lord at all times: his praise shall continually be in my mouth. My soul shall make her boast in the Lord: the humble shall hear thereof and be glad. O magnify the Lord with me and let us exalt his name together. I sought the Lord, and He heard me, and delivered me from all my fears" (Psalms 34:1-4 kjv).
>
> Believe me, God can do a much better job handling people than you could ever attempt to do.

FEAR OF STEPPING OUT

I have a question. Do you have the fear of the unknown? Are you afraid or hesitate to even think about what is to come perhaps tomorrow? If so, then you are not alone. Millions of people every day go about their daily activities living each moment as it comes. In other word's they live not only day to day but moment to moment. Living a life on eggshells and being afraid to move forward can be worrisome and cause you to live a life full of anxiety and stress.

I once met a guy he must have been in his late forties or fifties. We sat on a bench outside our cars waiting for our spouse to get off work. We began to talk about our children. He mentioned that his son had just finished grad school and was about to begin his life as a lawyer. He had taught his son at an early age how to make plans and set future goals and his son was right on track from elementary all the way through grad school. He was so proud of his son. As we talked further, he began to start talking about his own life how he at one time wanted to go to college but somewhere along the way he got distracted. He was a little hesitant at the time to leave his parent's house and neighborhood friends behind. He felt that he was smart enough to go to college and came up with about ten different excuses as to why he did not go.

After about an hour when he finally finished talking, he held his head down and took in a deep breath and said:

"Actually sir, I was simply afraid to step out because I did not know what to expect by attending college. I had the perfect opportunity, school tuition was totally paid for, had a car, no excuses. During that time of my life I could have went on to college and if I failed, I could have at least said that I tried." Our wives came out and we left the parking lot leaving me not even responding and never seeing him again. That is OK because I do not think he was ready to hear my hesitations in life.

Being afraid of stepping out on faith kept him from not only going to college but possibly effecting his personal future. How can one decision, one moment in life where we hesitated, can completely alter everything? Sometime we just gotta take a chance and step out on faith. If you fail hey, at least you can say that you tried and gave it your all. It will be ok, if things don't turn out the way you expected or the way you planned at least you can say that you tried, right?

FEAR OF THE UNKNOWN

It is no doubt that one day, we all at one time in our life are going to leave this world. We live each day hopefully in a life that is pleasing to the Lord. But, do we ever think about what happens after we die, where we will spend eternity? Fact is that a lot of people simply refuse or is trying not to even think about it.

I am a chaplain working at the local hospital. I do rounds speaking to patients. Since I was a previous dialysis patient, I found it very rewarding speaking to and encouraging patients who were going through the very same issues I went through and overcame, letting them know that if I could make it so could they.

I came across this one patient who was also being visited by several of their family members. The daughter had spoken to me ahead of time and said that their mom had just started dialysis and was on the verge of giving up on life. She asked if I could talk to her. When I entered the room, the elderly lady looked at me with the saddest and most terrified face I have ever seen.

Based on my previous many years as a dialysis patient myself and the experience of being in a coma, I felt that we could relate to each other. She felt that she had lived a good life but was not ready to start dialysis and would continue living her life without it. I spoke to her and told her of my situation how I had been a dialysis patient for over thirty years and the different obstacle's that I had to overcome but by the grace of God I am still here. God had a plan for me that I needed to achieve in life. I spoke to her and told her that God has work for her to do and that dialysis was not the end of the world nor a death sentence. I could still feel a sense of confusion on her mind as she looked at me with a half-smile. What do you do when you don't know what to do? You call upon the name of the Lord! We prayed for some time and after about an hour she finally smiled as she began to get encouraged.

When her daughter entered the room, she jumped, smiled and yelled "Mom!" She clapped her hands when she saw her Mother for the first time in a while finally smiling. After that, I felt it was time for me to leave. To her daughter's surprise, as I was leaving, her mother sat up in the bed with a big smile and said, "What is your name again? Thank you for stopping by and talking with me." Sometimes all a person need is a prayer and a few words of encouragement to keep them pressing forward.

So, in general terms, how do we overcome the spirit of fear? The fear of the unknown, fear of change, fear of people, fear of getting ill or sick, how do we overcome the spirit of fear? Believe me when I tell you that raising three daughters in this world was not easy. Feelings of fear often tried to take over my mind. There were days that I wanted to give up and throw in the towel. But I had to remember the prophesy that was placed over our home:

"As for me and my house, We will serve the Lord" (Josh. 24:2-15 kjv).

We actually had to fight for that prophesy to come to pass. Wife and I prayed and cried out to the Lord every day and night and declared:

* Satin, you will not take our family!
* Satin, you have no hold on our finances!
* We will serve You LORD!

The Bible says in the book of Ephesians

(Eph 6:10-18 kjv) to:

"Put on the Whole Amour of God, that ye may be able to stand against the wiles of the devil. For we wrestle not against flesh and blood, but against principalities, against powers, against the rulers of the darkness of this world, against spiritual wickedness in high places" (Eph. 6:1 kjv).

But, how do we do that? How do we put on the Whole Amour of God?

How do we stand therefore having our loins gird about with truth, and having on the Breastplate of righteousness?

How do we Shod our feet with the preparation of the gospel?

How do we above all take on the Shield of faith, wherewith we may be able to quench all the fiery darts of the wicked?

How do we put on the Helmet of salvation, and how do we use the Sword of the spirit?

Main question is how do we stand or fight against things we cannot even see? The answer is through, Prayer!

When you put on the Breastplate of righteousness, you pray for the righteousness of God for protection over your life. Not only over your personal life but also over those around you.

When we Shod our feet, we pray, we are praying for peace. You may wonder how does the word **peace** relate to **shoes**? The word "**gospel**" means "good news" referring to the sacrifice Jesus made for us that we may be saved. This in result brings us much needed **peace**. Having our feet fitted with shoes of the **gospel of peace** always allows us to be always ready to share the good news of the gospel with others. The shoes of peace equip us to fight for Christ in the spiritual battles we may face.

When you take on the Shield of faith, we hold onto our faith like a shield. So, when you encounter things like unbelief, sickness, doubt we hold tightly on to our belief and our faith.

When we were the Helmet of Salvation, we are protecting ourselves spiritually from a powerful blow of doubt from the enemy and protects us from a spiritual death. We put on the helmet of salvation by staying in the scriptures and reading God's Word every day.

When we carry the Sword of the spirit, we are carrying the Word of God which is the Holy Bible. We need to be knowledgeable in the Word of God and know how to use it against the enemy. Knowing God's Word in our heart keeps us prepared for anything.

Let me ask you a question. How are you going to be able to use the God given authority you have against the enemy if you don't what power you have? How can you exercise the God given benefits you have without reading the Bible? This brings to mind when I learned a lesson from not reading first

There was a time when I had brought my first smart television. I was thrilled and excited watching all the new stations and at what my remote could do. Actually, I was so satisfied that I threw the box along with all those unnecessary papers that came with it in the closet and shut the door. When my middle daughter Jocelyn returned home, who loves to read went into the closet to get something she saw what I had thrown away. She began to start reading the manual that came with the television. "Daddy, did you know that television allows you to video chat with relatives? Did you know that you can watch up to five stations at the same time on that television?" She named over fifteen different benefits that came with the television that I was not even aware of simply because I failed to read the manual.

It is important that you continually reading the manual, The Holy Bible!

Fear is death, but faith is your future! Increase your faith and you can overcome your fears.

Prayer:

Dear heavenly father of heaven and earth, I thank you Lord for all forgiveness. I thank you for delivering me from the spirit of fear. I have been afraid of so many things in my life and I thank you for deliverance. lord, You have given me strength and I am no longer a captive of being fearful of people, fear of money, fear of the unknown. I know that you are the King of kings and lord of lords.

I will trust you and I will see the goodness of the Lord., I will continue to seek you and I will not be afraid anymore. I pour my heart out to you lord. Your love will sustain and keep me through anything, You are my light and salvation and I will never fear again! In Jesus Name I pray, Amen.

Reflection and Chapter Questions

1. What do you consider as fear?
2. What experience in life has caused you to become fearful? Ex: fear of water, darkness, people etc.
3. How did you face the fear to overcome it?
4. What things are you doing at the present time to help others to overcome fear?
5. What are the most important issues the churches are facing today?

RSEARCH QUESTION:

In this chapter Paul talks about putting on the Whole Armor of God. Which of the Whole Armors of God do we use to protect our hearts?

Note: You can find the answer at the end of the book

CHAPTER 12

FORGIVENESS

"Forbearing one another, and forgiving one another, if any man have a quarrel against any: even as Christ forgave you, so also do ye."

--- (Col. 3:13 kjv)

Why does it always seem like the ones whom you love the most are the ones who hurt you the most? The ones who can get so easily offended. The ones who are always the first to remind you of the negative issues of your past, are our very own family members. Why is that? Can you in your wildest dreams ever imagine yourself holding a grudge against someone for over thirty years? Not forgiving someone for something that happened to you that was so hurtful, so painful that every time you see that person, every time you even think about that person, a frown comes across your face all because of something that happened twenty or thirty years ago. You may not have seen that person in years, you may not have even heard that person's name come up in conversation in years but one thing you do know is that-I don't like them and I don't forgive them for

> For if ye forgive men their trespasses, your heavenly Father will also forgive you: But if ye forgive not men their trespasses, neither will your Father forgive your trespasses (Matthew 6:14-15 kjv).

what they did to me! Believe me when I tell you that unforgiveness opens up the door to bitterness. The longer you hold on to unforgiveness and bitterness, the longer it will take for you to let it go.

"Looking diligently lest any man fail of the grace of God; lest any root of bitterness springing up trouble, and by this many become defiled" (Hebrew 12:15 kjv).

Sometimes it can be a lack of communication or simply a misunderstanding of the situation: you are thinking things one way and the other person is thinking the same thing from a totally different perspective. The difference is that, you are suffering trying to remember all the details of the incident while the other person have forgotten all about it and have gone on with their life. Believe me, it happens.

Sad thing about the previous couple of sentences is that, you probably yourself don't even remember what initially caused you to feel the way you do or the main reason as to why you refuse to forgive them. Forgiving someone can sometimes be a hard pill to swallow especially when the hurt has been embedded deep within your heart for so long that even when you try to forgive, it seems almost Impossible. The Bible states that we should never let the sun go down on our anger or give the devil an opportunity to step in our heart.

Unforgiveness begins at home. The bottom line is that you must first forgive yourself and only then can you truly start to forgive others, it begins with you.

So, what are some of the benefits of forgiveness?

*When you truly forgive someone, your fellowship with the Father will be allowed to flow freely.

*When you truly forgive someone, it prevents the devil from stepping in and inflicting torture and pain on you.

I once heard in a sermon where the preacher said that "holding unforgiveness in your heart causes the heart to become harden and oft times makes you feel bitter not only towards that particular person who hurt you but you also begin to develop indirect forms of resentment towards others affiliated with the person who hurt you who has absolutely nothing to do with the issue at hand."

I, at one time in my youthful years once joined an organization where I was maybe twenty or so years of age. Most of the other members were in their forties and up around my father's age. When it came to voting in new members one particular member would on occasion stand up and say something to the fact that "If you know someone who is so terrible, so unfit and not worthy to become a member of this organization, then just maybe you need to take a look at yourself and just maybe you might find that they are not the problem but you are." That statement stuck with me for a long time. Do we really know someone who is that bad of a person who is that unworthy of your forgiveness? Who are you to judge? Where is your heart? I thought that we as Christians in the body of Christ are supposed to be the ones who are setting an example for unbelievers to follow.

What would it take for you to take up your cross and go to someone and say, "I forgive you?" They may not even have a clue as to what you are referring to and you should not have to go into great detail but simply say "I forgive you." I promise you that will take a huge hidden burden off of you and you will begin to feel a brand-new sense of release and peace will come upon you. Do you really have a heart of forgiveness or for that matters do you even desire a forgiving heart?

Sometimes, we just need hear a person out and listen to what they have to say before issuing judgement and making a decision because they just might have a legitimate excuse for what they did and a legitimate reason for their actions.

Years ago, there was a man who had just purchased his first brand new car. It was an all red sports car took right off the showcase floor.

He got on the highway and wanted to test it out to see what it could do. Ten miles over the speed limit, fifteen miles over the speed limit. As he drove over a hill there awaiting him was a State Trooper. The State Trooper got behind the man and he began to drive faster and faster. The State Trooper turned on his lights and by the time the State Trooper finally caught up with him, the man was driving well over the twenty-five miles over the speed limit!

The State Trooper eventually pulled him over and walked over to the driver's side. The State Trooper looked at the man in the car and asked, "Do you know why I pulled you over?" The man just nodded his head.

The exhausted State Trooper said:

"Look here, it is at the end of my shift, I am tired, and I am ready to go home. I tell you what, if you can give me a unique excuse. One that I have never heard before in my life, a reason as to why you were driving so fast driving away from me, I will let you off of this one-hundred-dollar ticket that I am about to give to you."

The man held his head down and said:

"Truthfully, sir, my wife recently left me and ran off with a State Trooper and I thought you were trying to catch up with me to give her back."

The State Trooper without even saying a word just got back into his patrol car and drove off. Sometimes you simply need to get a clear understanding of a situation before making judgement.

Before harboring preconceived notions in your heart towards someone please consider this, "What would Jesus do" in this situation or "How would the Father handle this matter?" Believe me, God can take care of a person and handle any situation a whole lot better than any of us could. Have you ever considered why a person said what they said or the reason as to why they did what they did?

> When you truly understand the nature of a person, you will never be surprised by their actions or behavior.

Years ago, while attending college, I had a roommate who came from the city of Chicago. We lived in the dorm room together for over two years. His name was Sam and my first impression of him was overwhelming. Here I was dressed in a tee shirt and jeans. Sam came to college in a suit, tie and he carried a briefcase! I have to admit it, he was sharp. I was a peaceful person able to get along with everyone. Actually, it took a whole lot for me to get angry not to mention fighting but my roommate Sam was different. That first day in our dorm room we talked, and we learned about each other. Over time, Sam's natural behavior began to start showing. He was not only becoming disrespectful to other classmates but also towards professors. Within the first couple of months, Sam had gotten into three fights, many augments and all it took was for someone to say one wrong word to him to set him off. People really did not understand Sam as to why he was behaving the way he was. Yes, we were young adults and we were expected to carry ourselves in a respectable manner.

Sam had a hard attitude but there were times when we would sit up late and just talk. We talked about our upbringing as a child and I mentioned that I was from Cincinnati Ohio, each of my parents had good jobs, we lived in a nice clean neighborhood and I attended one of the top high schools in the state. I got good grades and had lots of friends.

Sam began to tear up as he began to talk about his childhood growing up in Chicago. He explained that he lived in a crowded two-bedroom apartment with his mom, sister and one other brother. Sam was only ten, his sister was seven and his little brother was only four when they lost their Dad in a gun fight. Times were hard for the family. The sound of gun shots and ambulances was a natural sound. Fights occurred outside their door and out on the streets on a daily basis. Sam joined a street gang at the age of eleven where stealing, robbing and even killing was a natural way of survival.

Sam's mom had to leave him and his siblings in the house by themselves every day to go off to work. There were many days where there was no food to eat and they all even Sam's mom went hungry.

Sam looked and asked me, "Do you see that briefcase that I brought to college with me?"

I said "yes."

Sam said, "You will never guess how or where I got it from."

I said, "How."

Sam said, "Before I got on the airplane to get here, there was a bomb scare at the airport. When security secured the airport, they ripped open this briefcase. They found nothing and threw the case in the garbage. After everything had settled down, I took the briefcase out of the garbage, taped it up and here it is. You see this suit I am wearing, my mom got it from the free store the day before I left home."

I have to tell you my reader, sometimes you think your situation is so terrible until that moment when you hear someone else's situation.

I clearly remember the first day of college classes where Sam and I took together. The teacher asked the class to explain some of the hardest times they experienced as a child growing up. One student said that it was hard for the family when their father lost his job, another stated that they at one time did not have a car. One girl stood up crying and said that she absolutely hated having to cook for the entire family every day. She had to prepare meals every day, she felt like she was being treated like Cinderella and she was fed up and tired of it.

Sam stood up and asked the girl "You mean you ate every day?"

Sometimes we think that our life is so terrible until the moment when you step into someone else's shoes. I understood Sam's nature and background regarding him fighting, his upbringing and his terrible language and quick temper which explained his actions and behavior. This also made it easy for me to forgive him for a lot of the things he did to me. Before any of us can judge or place preconceived notions upon anybody, it might be best that you get to know them first. You might just find out that they were nothing like the person who you thought they were. Do not let the spirit of unforgiveness hold you back.

Let us pray:

"Father, I ask that you deliver me from the spirit of unforgiveness that dwells in my heart. Please, come into my heart and instill in me joy, peace, and love as only you can give. I repent for all the negative thoughts and feelings I have towards_____and I ask for forgiveness. Please open new doors for me and give me a new heart and lease on life. I now release _____ from the bondage of unforgiveness, in Jesus name I pray, Amen."

My friend, through your prayer, the Lord has opened up your heart to view people and situations from a totally different aspect. The heart of forgiveness allows you to live your life to the fullest. Your mind is clearer, and you are more able to forgive others but, more importantly more able to forgive yourself.

Reflection and Chapter Questions

1. Explain in what ways have you been hurt the most in your life.

2. Do you feel deep down that you have a problem forgiving someone?
3. What are your main obstacles or reasons preventing you from forgiving them?
4. How has the Spirit of Pride affected your life?
5. How do you approach someone and ask for forgiveness?

RSEARCH QUESTION:

What sin does the Bible consider to be unforgiven?
Note: You can find the answer at the end of the book

CHAPTER 13

RELENTLESS FAITH

Therefore, my beloved brethren, be ye steadfast, unmovable, always abounding in the work of the Lord, forasmuch as ye know that your labour is not in vain in the Lord.

---1 Cor. 15:58 kjv

I have a question. When you think about the days of Moses. When it came time for Moses and the Israelites to cross the Red Sea, Pharaoh's army pursuing them on one side and the mighty Red Sea on the other side, who do you think at that time had the most faith?

Was it Moses? He led the Israelites out of the land of Egypt to the Red Sea.

Was it the Pharaoh of Moses who was cruel and vindictive or his army whose only intent was to destroy the Israelites?

Out of the thousands of people in Egypt, Who do you think had the most faith? I will tell you this much, it was not Moses. It was not Pharaoh or anybody in his army.

The person who had the most faith in this situation was that one person who took that first step into the Red Sea. That person who had no clue what to expect. Did not know how close Pharaoh's army was to them. Did not know if the mighty waters of the Red Sea would swallow everyone up and drown everybody. He did not even know if he would be all by himself and the only one to step into the Red Sea. But, one thing he did know and that was this, he knew that by faith he had to step out into that Red Sea even if he had to go all by himself and if he had to be the first one to dive in!

Many days in our lives we have to do things and make choices not knowing if the decision was a right or wrong one or even more or less considering the outcome. Everyone has some form of level of faith and that faith can affect the way we live. Our spiritual life depends on the level of faith we have not only in ourselves but more importantly in God.

> "For I say, through the grace given unto me, to every man that is among you, not to think of himself more highly than he ought to think; but to think soberly, according as God hath dealth to every man the measure of faith"(Rom. 12:3 kjv).

It seems to me like a lot of people had more faith when they were younger than what they presently have today. What happened during your lifetime to cause your level of faith especially in The Lord to decline? Was it a bad breakup, was it an unexpected illness or perhaps the loss of a loved one?

Out of all the many test and trials that I have experienced in my life such as a near death experience, comatose, various hospital test, raising a family and so on, I had no choice but to put my total trust and faith not in the doctors, not the pastors, not the medicines but in God alone!

Every battle that I had to overcome, every road that I had to cross, every burden that I had to bear, every trial that I had to face head on, each and every last one of them increased my faith in God tremendously.

So, what exactly is faith? The Bible describes faith like this: "Faith cometh by hearing and by hearing the Word of God" or "Faith is the substance of things hoped for, evidence of things not seen" or "We walk by faith, not by sight." In simple terms, believing without evidence.

I can describe faith from my own experience like this: Doing or acting upon something without any experience or knowledge of the work that needs to be done in completing a task in the hopes of a positive outcome.

Wife and I had three children at a young age not knowing or having any childbearing experience. We attended college not knowing where the next quarters tuition was going to come from. Truthfully, my wife and I did a lot of things going strictly by faith.

In the year 2017, we actually drove our cars from Ohio to Texas (1000 miles) not knowing anything about the area we were moving into, we did not have a job and the house we were having built was not yet completed! Talk about stepping out on faith? Living a true life of faith means living beyond not so much as your means but beyond your expectations, living beyond what you or anyone else thinks you are capable of achieving.

There are so many normal people in the Bible who depended on their faith and eventually overcame, I will list to you my dear reader just a few:

*Abraham: When Abraham was ninety-nine years old and Sarah his wife was well over ninety years of age well past child barring years, God promised her a son. Abraham actually fell on his face and laughed in his heart thinking it was impossible for his wife to have a child. He said in his heart, "for shall a child be born unto him that is a hundred years old and shall Sarah, that is ninety years old, bear"? God did bear them both several sons and the first son was named Isaac. Gen. 21:1-3 kjv

*Joshua: When God told Joshua that the land of Jericho was in their hands and if he and the children of Israel compassed round about the city of Jericho

seven days the walls of that city would fall flat. Joshua had faith in God's word and followed instructions. On the seventh day, they compassed around about the city of Jericho six times and on the seventh day, after compassing about the city seven times the walls of Jericho did fall flat and they destroyed everything that was in the city.

(Jos. 6:20 kjv)

Noah: During the days of Noah, the human race was full of wickedness, corruption and the thought of their hearts was full of evil, God told Noah to build an Ark because he was going to wipe out the human race with a flood which also included animals, birds and every creature. Noah had faith in God's word and built the ark. On the seventh day, God sent rain and it rained for forty days and forty nights. Flood waters came upon the earth and everything was destroyed except for the people and animals inside the Ark (Gen 6:8-10 kjv).

Being obedient is not doing something that you want to do. Obedience is doing something that you have to do perhaps following instructions as in given in the prior examples of Abraham, Joshua, and Noah. They were being obedient because they heard from the Lord and acted upon His instructions.

I have been truly blessed to be baptized and filled with the Holy Spirit with evidence of speaking in tongues many years ago. Living a life of relentless faith is so awesome and going through life I have learned to be more patient and to put my trust in God. I have gotten to a point in my life that when I try to do things or fulfill works of the flesh, many times it really becomes frustrating. Works of the flesh means doing our own will and not God's. Get out of the works of the flesh because it never produces anything so put your trust and faith in God alone. Whatever level of faith in God you presently have my dear reader, it can always be increased. When your faith in God is truly relentless, your faith is unwavering, unmovable, unchangeable, and unshakable. After all my trials, I could only say, "Thank You, Jesus for seeing me through!" Thanking God after something has happened is called <u>Gratitude</u>. Thanking God before something happens is called <u>Faith</u>! Live by Faith my Sisters and Brothers!

Reflection and Chapter Questions

1. When was that one time in your life when you had to depend on your faith alone?
2. How has your faith improved over the years and made you a better person?
3. What areas in your life are you most faithful?
4. In this chapter, Paul talks about the Holy Spirit. Explain how has the Holy Spirit helped you to be more faithful in life?
5. Who or what do you do you depend on to help you to remain positive in difficult situations?
   a. What personal lesson can you learn from the examples of Abraham, Joshua, and Noah?

RSEARCH QUESTION:

Who baptized Jesus?
Note: You can find the answer at the end of the book

CHAPTER 14

I AM THE LORD WHO HEALS YOU!

"And said, If thou wilt diligently hearken to the voice of the Lord thy God, and wilt do that which is right in his sight, and wilt give ear to his commandments, and keep all his statutes, I will put none of these diseases upon thee, which I have brought upon the Egyptians: for I am the Lord that healeth thee."

Exodus 15:26 kjv

When I first read this verse, I realized that the Lord had given us clear instructions as to what we need to do in order to be healed! It simply says to call upon the elders of the church and let them pray with faith over you, anoint you with oil and then the Lord shall raise them up. Wow, and if you had committed any sins they would be forgiven. That is one direct and powerful statement! Working as a chaplain I would on occasional go to the chapel and pray before going to my assigned floor to visit the patients. One visit I clearly remember was with a man to be about seventy or so years of age.

When I entered the room, I could clearly see that his spirits were down, and it looked as though he had given up on life. I sat on a chair next to his bed and asked how he was doing? He looked at me and said, "Don't you already know?" I said, "No, I did not look at your charts." Well the man said, "I have a serious case of pneumonia, my body is very sick, and I don't have any family or get any visitors." I listened patiently and by the time he finished talking he had given me about fifteen different reasons as to why he was feeling sick. I simply asked him, "Do you believe that God can heal you?"

The man looked at me with a surprised expression and said, "Are you for real?" I said "Yes." With a smile on his face, he looked at me and said, "Sure."

Now, I was always taught in the chaplains training classes to never give false hope to patients by telling them something totally different from what the doctors had been advising them of. I am very careful and aware not to do that, but I do believe in the powerful healing of God

> I will therefore that men pray everywhere, lifting up holy hands, without wrath and doubting (1Tim.2:8 kjv).

and that He can do anything. I asked the man in the bed if he would like for me to pray for him and he agreed. For several minutes or so I prayed not so much for healing but a prayer of faith over him. As I was praying a nurse entered the room and when she noticed that we were praying to my surprise she raised her hands and started praying as well. When we eventually finished praying, we opened our eyes and realized that the nurse had fallen to her knees crying and weeping. The man in the bed looked at me and I looked at him and we both had a big question mark expression on our face.

The nurse got up and said that she had been waiting all day for someone, anyone to come to the floor and would offer prayers for the patients. She wiped the tears from her eyes and then said that she was the one who was in dire need of prayers. She was in the process of filing bankrupt and was about to lose her

> The effectual fervent prayer of a righteous man availeth much. (James 5:16 kjv

home. She said that after we had finished praying that her faith was lifted and that she felt that she could go on. She left the room without even taking the man's vital signs! The man in the bed looked at me and said that he also felt much better and that after being in the hospital for a whole week that was the first time anyone had actually prayed for him. I asked if he needed anything from the Chaplain Department and he said "No, but thank you for the prayers."

> Beloved, I wish above all things that thou mayest prosper and be in health, even as thy soul prospered. 3 John 1:2 kjv

I left out the room and noticed the nurse who had come in the room. She came down from the nurse's station and gave me a big hug and said, "Thank you, please don't stop coming to this floor, we need all the prayers we can get." I said, "OK." That was my first patient visit for that day, but I felt that God's purpose and plan for me being there at that moment and time had been fulfilled. I had intentions of praying for the patient, but God had a different plan and knew the nurse was the one who needed prayer the most. She was the one who's faith needed to be healed. When the man in the bed was asked "do you want to be healed", his response was, "sure." To me, his response showed a lack of belief and no real desperation in any form of him wanting to be healed!

God knows our heart and He knows where our level of faith in healing stands. When you come to the realization that Jesus is our healer, you do not put so much faith in doctors, medicines, or anyone, just trust in the Lord!

We see even in the Bible where certain ones needing a healing turned away from God because they felt that the physicians were their best option. You remember King Asa, the third king of Judah. Well,

> "For I am the Lord who heals you." (Exodus 15:26 kjv)

King Asa was a godly king, but during the end of his life, He had come down with a disease of the feet, probably similar to what we call today as gout that left him in severe pain. I can tell you my dear reader about gout because I suffered from it years ago and it is very painful especially, in the toes.

In his early life, King Asa's ultimate intent was to have military success but in reality, during his later years he had become a failure spirituality when he turned to the physicians instead of God for his feet getting healed (2 Chron. 16:1-12 kjv).

Now, this does not mean that you should stop taking medicines or consulting with your doctors, but we should always pray on things first. Remember that all healings come from God whether He sends his anointing through a doctor, nurse, or anyone else because God can give wisdom and anointing to doctors to perform their duties.

Throughout my years, I have actually seen with my own eyes doctors and nurses huddling in corners and praying together before performing major surgeries. But God gets all the glory and honor because He is God and He alone provides all of our needs. We serve a miracle working God, and He can heal you! If you confess the Lord, just call Him up! Tell Him what you want! While you are trying to figure things out, busting your brain trying to decide between two issues, depriving yourself of sleep constantly asking yourself, "Lord, what shall I do?" Look here, just call Him up and tell Him what you want! Don't you know that He has an answer to the question before you even ask.

> And In that day ye shall ask me nothing. Verily, Verily, I say unto you, Whatsoever ye shall as the Father in my name, he will give it you. Hitherto have ye asked nothing in my name: ask, and ye shall receive, that your joy may be full. John 16:23-24 kjv

The Lord is waiting on you. He asked Ezekiel, "Can these bones live?" He asked a lame man, "Will thou be made whole?" God is asking you today, "My child, what will you ask God for today?" God will answer you!

God already knows the answer and what is in our heart but sometimes will ask us a question so that we can think. So, while you are making yourself sick causing yourself to become depressed by worrying, God has already figured out the solution and outcome. He is waiting for you to simply ask. God knows our beginning and our ending. Jesus knows that it may get hard at times but, in the midnight hour when everybody has left and you are all alone, He will hold you, when the storms of life come upon you like a whirlwind, He will comfort you and give you peace! It does not matter what time of day it is morning, noon, or evening, or in the midnight hour, just call on Him,

"JESUS, I NEED YOU, I LOVE YOU, I WILL SERVE YOU!"

"He is truly the only one who can give complete joy, healing, peace, comfort because He is the King of the universe and owns it all. Just call Him up and He will answer you, that's not something I said, that's what JESUS said!

Prayer:

Lord Jesus, I am in need of a healing. I have suffered long enough, and I am tired! My body is tired, my mind is tired and Lord, I feel hopeless many days. I know that you can heal me, and I am turning to you. Lord, You are my only hope. I am calling upon you right now to please have mercy on me. I repent of my sins and I ask for forgiveness. Please hear my cry Oh Lord, You are my only hope. Please touch my body and heal me, in Jesus name I pray, amen.

Reflection and Chapter Questions

1. Is there a particular verse in the bible that you refer to regarding healing?
2. Who or what do you depend on most for when it comes to a bodily healing? A spiritual healing? Ex: doctors, medicines, church leader, your faith.
3. Has there ever been a time in your life when you experienced a divine or instant healing?
4. How do you pray for others when they are in need of a healing from God?

5. In this chapter we talked about King Asa. In the beginning of his life he was a Godly man and relied on God for everything. What event or events turned him around to where he all of a sudden began to start relying on physicians?

RSEARCH QUESTION:

Besides Jesus, who else in the Bible preformed miracles?
Note: You can find the answer at the end of the book

CHAPTER 15

BE READY

Therefore, be ye also ready: for in such an hour as
ye think not the Son of man cometh
(Matthew 24:44 kjv).

With the recent worldwide outbreak of the virus covid-19, with
the world on the brink of unprecedented famine, the world suffering
from racial unrest and Earthquakes occurring in places like never
before, can't you see that these are the signs of the times? Can't you
see that the coming of the Lord is near? Just in this past year alone,
the nation has been taught to not stand or be too close to anyone and
to distant ourselves from each other. Just in this past year alone, the
nation has been racially separated more than ever.

Just in this past year alone The United States unemployment
levels rates fell to 13.3 percent in May 2020 from 14.7% in 1939
which was previously the record
established during the Great
Depression. At the same time, we are
saying that we are in the process of
making the nation great again. I don't think that our nation or even
the world is in its condition because of bad decisions of leaders or
ones who are experienced in a particular area of such but in reality,

> Be ye also patient; stablish
> your hearts: for the coming of
> the Lord draweth nigh
> (James 5:8 kjv).

these are signs that the Lord is giving us that his soon coming is near. The Bible says "nation will rise up against nation, and kingdom against kingdom, earthquakes, famines and pestilences in various places, persecution, betrayal, hatred, signs in the sun, moon and stars and that men will faint from terror but Christians will recognized these signs as a warning of Jesus coming"

(Luke21:7-15 kjv).

Are you paying attention to what the Bible says? Are you preparing yourself for that glorious day?

> "Now when these things begin to take place, straighten up and rise your heads, because your redemption is drawing near" (Luke 21:18 ESV).

> *God told Ezekiel to Get ready; prepare yourself (Ez.38:7 KJV).
> *God says that He is going to prepare a place for you (John 14:3 KJV).

We find so many instances in the Bible where God speaks and talks about preparation and preparing yourself. My question to you is "Are you ready for the coming of the Lord?" If the Lord appeared right now, would you consider yourself as being ready? Will the Lord say to you, "Well done thy good and faithful servant" at your appearance before Him?" Many people really believe that they are ready for the coming of Christ, but in reality, many of us probably are not.

I have found that through my years a lot of people feel that by doing good things throughout life such as being kind or polite to people or in some instances they can earn their way into heaven. But God did not call us to do good things, He has called us to do Good Works. There is a big difference between doing good things and doing Good Works. When you do good things, it is probably for the benefit of another person or yourself. When you do Good Works, God is in the midst of it. The fact of the matter is that many of us try to do things for Jesus, but we fail to do things with Jesus! Meaning that we all so often attempt do things in our own strength. The kingdom belongs to Jesus. Ministers how can you minister to others without Him and His love? Remember that we are not saved by doing good works though because before we are saved, our works are done in the flesh. We can only be saved through God's grace and mercy!

> Jesus saith unto him, I am the way, the truth, and the life: no man cometh unto the Father, but by me.
> John 14:6 KJV

So, what does it mean to prepare yourself or to be ready, especially when it comes to preparing ourselves and being ready for the coming of the Lord? We see in the bible where a servant was confused about being born again and being ready for the coming of Christ.

We read in the book of John that there was a man named Nicodemus who was a man of the Pharisees and a ruler of the Jews: The same came to Jesus by night, and said unto him, "Rabbi, we know that thou art a teacher come from God: for no man can do these miracles that thou doest, except God be with him"(John 3:2 kjv).

Jesus answered and said unto him, "Verily, verily, I say unto thee, Except a man be born again, he cannot see the kingdom of God" (John 3:3 kjv).

Nicodemus saith unto Jesus, "How can a man be born when he is old? can he enter the second time into his mother's womb, and be born?" (John 3:4 kjv). Here you can see that Nicodemus did not clearly understand what Jesus was trying to say to him, so Jesus had to break it down.

Jesus answered, "Verily, verily, I say unto thee, Except a man be born of water and the Spirit, he cannot enter into the kingdom of God. That which is born of the flesh is flesh; and that which is born of the Spirit is spirit. Marvel not that I say unto thee, Ye must be born again." (John 3:5-6 KJV)

The NIV version of this same scripture says it like this: "Jesus answered him" referring to Nicodemus, "I tell you the truth, no one can enter the kingdom of God unless he is born of water and the spirit. Flesh gives birth to flesh, but the Spirit gives birth to spirit. You should not be surprised at my saying; You must be born again." At this point Jesus is not only speaking to Nicodemus but to us all that we must be born again!

> Jesus answered and said unto him, Verily, Verily, I say unto thee, Except a man be born again, he cannot see the kingdom of God. John 3:3 NIV

Meaning you must be water baptized and experience a new birth referring to a spiritual rebirth. Once you have been baptized, you are now saved by grace. My dear ready, please be ready. The time is now to get your house in order, to get your children in order. Spread God's Word and tell people about the goodness of the Lord! The worst feeling in the world is to think that you made it into heaven, but your family did not.

Because we serve a patient God, He has given us time to prepare ourselves so that we can be ready. The best example my parents had shown to my Sister's and Brother's and I on preparing ourselves and being ready was something we did on a yearly basis and later on in life we all use those skills today to prepare ourselves a head of time especially for the coming of Christ when He returns.

> Watch ye therefore, and pray always, that ye may be accounted worthy to escape all these things that shall come to pass, and to stand before the Son of man (Luke 21:36 KJV).

When I was young and living at home with my parent's we often took trips out of state. It may have been a family reunion. It may have been a business trip. It may have been a vacation. Whatever the occasion or trip was my brother and I looked forward to for months ahead of time. If the trip was planned for the month of August, my Mom and Dad was planning five months ahead of time especially the fishing adventures.

My parents made sure that enough money was saved up, that we had appropriate clothing, that we had all the needed fishing equipment and that the hotel arrangements were made and confirmed so that when the time came for the trips, there were no surprises, we would be ready. Their knowledge of planning and thinking ahead of time made trips very pleasant. In the same way, we should always be ready and prepared for when Christ returns.

Are you planning your life and living in a way that is pleasing to the Lord? Go out and speak God's Word to everyone. Tell as many people about Christ as you can. We live in a world

> For I am not ashamed of the gospel of Christ: for it is the power of God unto salvation to ever one that believeth. Romans 1:16 KJV

where people are actually dying not ever hearing about Jesus Christ! Like I mentioned before, Get your house in order while you have time! Tomorrow is not promised to anyone! Will you be ready?

Prayer: Jesus Christ, I come to you with an open mind and heart. I thank you for being patient with me as I go through these difficult times in my life. I am ready for a change. I am tired of struggling, I am tired of the pain and I am tired of feeling that my life has no meaning. I repent for my sins and I ask for your forgiveness. I need help! I have tried the doctors; I have tried medicines, and nothing works. I need you Lord to step into my life and deliver me right now! I want to be ready for your soon coming. Please help me to be prepared! I need You in my life Lord! Please come into my life and help me to be ready!

In Jesus precious name I pray,

Amen.

Reflection and Chapter Questions

1. Have you been Born Again?
2. Have you Confessed and Repented of your sins?

3. Have you turned your life around and been baptized and washed in the blood of Jesus Christ?
4. Have you been tried in the fires and storms of life and overcame them or are you still struggling with them?
5. In what ways are you helping others to prepare for the coming of the Lord

RSEARCH QUESTION:

What did Jesus say will happen to those who shall endure unto the end?

Note: You can find the answer at the end of the book

CONCLUSION

None of the storms that you face or go through in life will ever be enjoyable and actually some may even be painful. God has never promised us that this life would be easy, but he did promise that no matter what storms we may face that He is working for our good and that He is much bigger than our struggles. No matter what storm you may have to endure, God says do not fear, He will always provide an out or a way to comfort you. How do I know? Well, because He said so.

> "But, now thus saith the Lord that created thee, O Jacob, and he that formed thee, O Israel, Fear not: for I have redeemed thee, I have called thee by name; thou art mine. When thou passest through the waters, I will be with thee; and through the rivers, they shall not overflow thee: when thou walketh through the fire, thou shalt not be burned; neither shall the flame kindle upon thee. For I am the Lord thy God, the Holy One of Israel, thy Savior: I gave Egypt for thy ransom, Ethiopia and Seba for thee" (Isaiah 43:1-3 KJV).

Some of the main reasons as to why it is of upmost importance that we overcome such things as depression, fear, doubt even having a spirit of unforgiveness is that when we overcome various storms in our life, we allow God to do a work in us.

When you overcome and open up your heart to God, He will:

1. Revile to you who He is: Corinthians 2:10
2. Revile to you, who you are: 1 Peter 2:9
3. Revile to you your purpose in life: Psalms 57:2
4. Revile to you the path you need to follow Him: Matt. 16:24

One thing is for sure and that is, if you can hold on just a little while longer. If you can endure until the end, God has a deliverance in store for you. The only person holding you back from fulfilling God's purpose for you, is you!

God says that:

> "Blessed is the man that endureth temptation: for when he is tried, he shall receive the crown of life, which the Lord hath promised to them that love Him" (James 1:12 KJV).

- He will give you strength for every battle (2Sam. 22:40 KJV).
- He will always protect you (2Thess. 3:3-5 KJV).
- He will forgive you even when you have sinned, (Matt. 6:14 KJV).

ENDING PRAYER

Dear Heavenly Father, my savior and my redeemer! I come to you with an open heart thanking You for always caring for me. You Lord are my deliverer and my healer. This day I confess my sins and I proclaim right now Father that:

* I close the door to, the spirit of bitterness and hate and let it be replaced with fire in my mouth!
* I close the door to, depression, and loneliness, and that my heart be replaced with the fire and anointing of God!
* I close the door to, the spirit of hopelessness and uselessness and it be replaced with the spirit of newness!
* I take authority over every evil spirit that has come up against me!
* I close the door to, the spirit of deceit and lust and that it is replaced with only the fulfillment of love from You Lord!
* I close the door to, the spiritual sickness and family problems.
* I declare this day that the Spirit of God will break every yoke and everything that is hindering me to move forward!

Today I take control over my life and I want You Jesus Christ to be the only door that will remain open in my heart and in my life! You are my Savior and my Redeemer! I love You Lord and I repent of every sin that I have ever committed and I ask for Your forgiveness. Please Lord continue to keep me under Your protective hands,

In Jesus name I pray, amen.

STEPS ON BECOMING AN OVERCOMER

1. You must first realize and have confidence in knowing that God will bring you through to victory and that He will hide His Word in your heart.
2. You must Recognize what is holding you back.
3. You must Develop a willingness to change.
4. Exercise your plan of attack
5. And then Celebrate the victory

THE SIGNS OF AN OVERCOMER

1. You are a Worshipper
2. You have a Spiritual Growth
3. You respect God's Word more.
4. You are more able to prioritize
5. You have learned from it
6. You recognize the issue and realize the victory
7. You have peace
8. You thank and praise God at a higher level

ANSWERS TO THE RESERCH QUESTIONS

1. <u>When Jesus said, "Get thee behind Me, Satin! For you are not mindful of the things of men." Who was Jesus speaking to?</u>

   Answer: Jesus was speaking to Peter because Peter was speaking for Satan. Jesus was trying to explain to His disciples that he had not come to establish an earthly Messianic kingdom at that time, Peter began to rebuke Jesus for having such a laidback mindset. Jesus said, "<u>Get behind Me, Satin! For you are not mindful of the things of men."</u> God knew that was not Peter speaking but Satan.

2. <u>Who did God speak to personally in the Bible?</u>

   Answer: Noah (Gen 6:13), Adam and Eve (Gen. 3:9-19 kjv), Abraham and his wife (Gen. 18 kjv).

3. <u>How was Job losing 7000 sheep detrimental to his burnt offerings?</u>

   Answer: "Job sent and sanctified his children, and rose up early in the morning, and offered burnt offerings according to the number of them all: for Job said, it may be that my sons have sinned, and cursed God in their hearts" (Job 1-5 kjv). Job made burnt offerings to God to protect his children spiritually. Losing burnt offerings was taking away a covering over his children.

4. <u>Why was Joseph so despised by his brothers?</u>

   Answer: The Bible says "Now Israel loved Joseph more than all his children, because he was the son of his old age: and he made him a coat of many colors" (Gen. 37:3 kjv). Joseph had dreams where his brother's wheat and even the sun, moon and stars were all "bowing down to him" (Gen. 37:4 kjv)

5. If God doesn't tempt us, why do you think that the Lord's prayer petition Him not to lead us into temptation?

    Answer: Actually, the phrase does not assume that God might lead us into temptation or tempt us but instead, it assumes that God does deliver us from temptation and evil. It gives the impression that temptation will come, but God will deliver evil from them.

6. What was the main reason as to why Herodias daughter (Salome: *name arrived from the historian Josephus*) asked for the head of John The Baptist?

    Answer: Actually, it was the idea of Herodias the mother. John the Baptist preached repentance because the kingdom of God is at hand and he condemned King Herod for divorcing his first wife and unlawfully marrying Herodias the wife of his half-brother Herod Philip which violated Mosaic Law (Matt. 14:1-2 kjv). Herodias was highly upset and used this occasion to get rid of John the Baptist by having him beheaded.

7. What is the main reason as to why Jeremiah was not allowed to marry by God?

    Answer: By not having children or taking a wife was a sign to the people of Judah that any children born in that land would suffer famine, die of grievous death (Jeremiah 16:2-4 kjv).

8. Why did King David arrange the death of Uriah the Hittite?

    Answer: King David had gotten Bathsheba pregnant and instead of repenting and confessing, David brought Uriah home from battle and insisted he sleep with Bathsheba therefore Uriah could assume to be the father. But

143

After Uriah refused, David plotted to have Uriah murdered. He sent Uriah back into the battle and put him on the front line where he died (2 Sam. 11:1-24 kjv).

9. We find that The Promise Land is mentioned in this chapter. Question is: Who are the only ones to who actually made it into The Promise Land?

    Answer: Caleb and Joshua because they have wholly followed the Lord. (Numbers 32:11-12 kjv).

10. What was the name of the person who first initiated the Hebrew's passage through the Red Sea, by walking in the sea Head-deep until the sea parted?

    Answer: Nahshon (according to a Jewish Midrash)

11. Which of the Whole Armors of God do we use to protect our hearts?

    Answer: The Breastplate of Righteousness (Eph. 6:14 kjv)

12. What does the Bible consider to be an unforgiven sin?

    Answer: Blasphemy against the Holy Ghost (Matt. 12:31 kjv).

13. Who was Jesus baptized by?

    Answer: Jesus was baptized by John The Baptist (Matt. 3:14 kjv)

14. Besides Jesus, who else in the Bible preformed miracles?

    Answer: Elijah and Elisha.

    Elijah performed a miracle when he "raised the dead" (1kings 17:22-23kjv), "Brought rain to end the drought" (1 Kings 18:41-45), Elijah also "parted the waters of the Jordan River" (2 Kings 2:8 kjv).

Elisha performed a miracle when he "purified water" (2 Kings 2:14 kjv), Elisha "raised a child from the dead" (2 Kings 4:32-37 kjv) and Elisha also "healed Naaman of leprosy" (2 Kings 5:1-19 kjv)

15. What do Jesus say will happen to those who endures and bears up under suffering to the end?

    Answer: Those who endures to the end shall be saved! (Matt. 10:22 kjv)

TO CONTACT THE AUTHOR

I pray that this book has been a blessing to you and through Christ Jesus has encouraged and strengthen you. I would love to hear from you and the battles you have overcome.

PLEASE WRITE:
Paul Phillips Jr.
457 Omaha Ave
Tyler, Tx 75704
Phillips772004@yahoo.com

"And the peace of God, which passeth all understanding, shall keep your hearts and minds through Christ Jesus," (Philippians 4:7 kjv).

MORE BOOKS BY THE AUTHOR

1. FROM TRIALS TO BLESSINGS
2. IN HIS PRESENCE
3. EMBRACED
4. THE PURPLE APPLE
5. RESERVATIONS FOR THE KINGDOM, PLEASE!

From Trials
To Blessings

by Paul Phillips

In His
Presence

Intimacy with the Father

PAUL PHILLIPS JR.

FOREWORD BY DONALD DANIELS

Embraced

The love that can only come from the Father

Paul Phillips

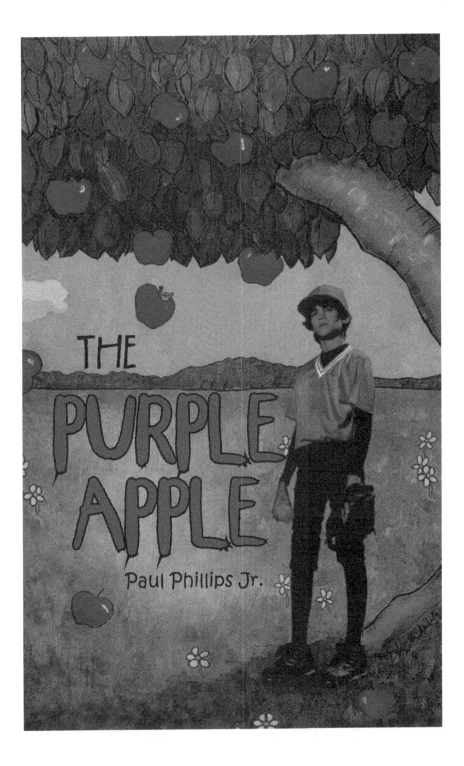

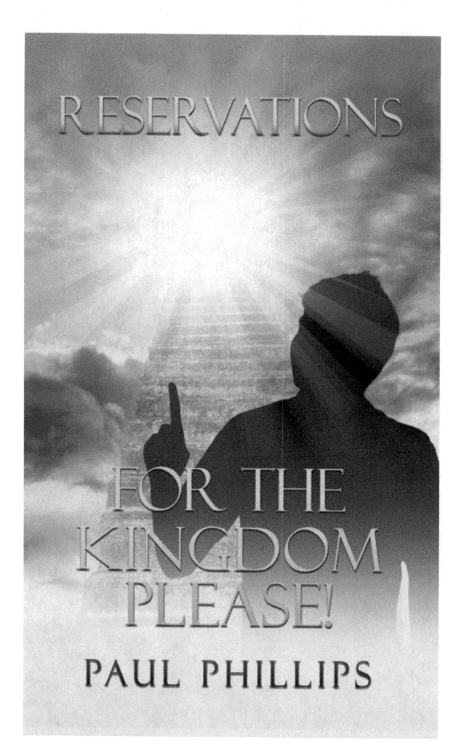

RESERVATIONS

FOR THE
KINGDOM
PLEASE!

PAUL PHILLIPS

Printed in the United States
By Bookmasters